WILD EDIBLE PLANTS OF THE PACIFIC NORTHWEST

LOCATE, IDENTIFY, STORE AND PREPARE YOUR FORAGED FINDS

FORAGED FINDS IN THE USA

SHANNON WARNER

© Copyright by Shannon Warner 2022 - All rights reserved.

The content contained within this book may not be reproduced, duplicated, or transmitted without direct written permission from the author or the publisher.

Under no circumstances will any blame or legal responsibility be held against the publisher, or author, for any damages, reparation, or monetary loss due to the information contained within this book. Either directly or indirectly. You are responsible for your own choices, actions, and results.

Legal Notice:

This book is copyright protected. This book is only for personal use. You cannot amend, distribute, sell, use, quote, or paraphrase any part, or the content within this book, without the author's or publisher's consent.

Disclaimer Notice:

Please note the information contained within this document is for educational and entertainment purposes only. All effort has been executed to present accurate, up-to-date, reliable, and complete information. No warranties of any kind are declared or implied. The author and Rowan's Publishing, LLC. are not medical professionals. It is essential to consult a healthcare professional before consuming plant or plant-based products, as some plants can be toxic or negatively interact with certain medications. Additionally, it is crucial to correctly identify plants before consuming them, as many poisonous plants can resemble edible plants. Always use caution and properly research any plant before consuming it.

By reading this document, the reader agrees that under no circumstances is the author responsible for any losses, direct or indirect, which are incurred as a result of the use of the information contained within this document, including, but not limited to, — errors, omissions, or inaccuracies.

ALSO BY SHANNON WARNER

Wild Edible Plants of the Mid-Atlantic

Wild Edible Plants of California

FLAVORS UNLEASHED

A THRILLING JOURNEY INTO THE PACIFIC NORTHWEST'S WILD EDIBLE WONDERLAND

The Pacific Northwest is known for its stunning natural beauty, with lush forests, rolling hills, and pristine coastlines that stretch as far as the eye can see. However, many people need to realize that this region is also home to a vast array of wild plants that have sustained Indigenous communities and settlers for centuries.

This book explores over 70 wild edible plants in the Pacific Northwest, including berries, nuts, greens, roots, and flowers. Each plant offers a unique taste and nutritional benefits, from the tart, bright-red berries of the huckleberry bush to the fragrant, nutty flavor of the hazelnut.

But foraging for wild plants isn't just about finding delicious food; it is also a way to connect with the natural world and learn about the rich history and culture of the Pacific Northwest. By harvesting these plants, we can better understand the land and the people who have lived here for generations.

However, as with any foraging activity, it is crucial to approach wild edible plants with respect and caution. Ethical and sustainable harvesting practices are essential to ensure that we don't harm the delicate balance of nature or over-harvest these precious resources. It is also essential to correctly identify the plants we are harvesting and to be aware of any potential safety concerns, such as poisonous look-a-likes or environmental contaminants.

But despite these potential challenges, foraging for wild edible plants can be a fun and rewarding activity for anyone who loves spending time outdoors and exploring the natural world. Whether you are a seasoned forager or just starting, this book is designed to be a comprehensive guide to the wild edible plants of the Pacific Northwest.

So, lace up your boots, and join us on a journey through the forests, fields, and coastlines of the Pacific Northwest as we discover the many delicious and nutritious wild edible plants this region offers.

PART ONE
FORAGING
FUNDAMENTALS
DISCOVERING AND SUSTAINING NATURE'S BOUNTY IN THE PACIFIC NORTHWEST

"One touch of nature makes the whole world kin."

-WILLIAM SHAKESPEARE

1 NATURE'S BUFFET
A BEGINNER'S GUIDE TO FORAGING IN THE PACIFIC NORTHWEST

Welcome to the exciting world of foraging, where the wonders of nature's pantry unfold before your very eyes! This beginner-friendly guide will equip you with the essential knowledge and skills to safely and confidently discover the bountiful wild edibles that await you in forests, meadows, and shores. From plant identification and harvesting techniques to foraging etiquette and safety tips, we've got you covered as you embark on your foraging adventures.

Embracing the Foraging Mindset:

Before setting out on your first foraging expedition, take a moment to cultivate a sense of curiosity, mindfulness, and appreciation for the natural world. Approaching foraging with an open, attentive mindset will enhance your overall experience and help you develop a deeper connection with the plants and ecosystems you explore.

Familiarize Yourself with Local Flora:

One of the most crucial aspects of foraging is learning to identify the plants you encounter accurately. Start by familiarizing yourself with your area's most common wild edibles, paying close attention to their unique characteristics, habitats, and growth patterns. Consider investing in a reliable field guide or joining a local foraging group to hone your plant identification skills.

Learn to Spot Lookalikes:

While many wild edibles are easy to identify, some closely resemble toxic or inedible plants. It's essential to learn the distinguishing features of these lookalikes to avoid accidental ingestion. Remember the golden rule of foraging: If you're not 100% sure of a plant's identity, don't eat it!

Safety First:

To ensure a safe and enjoyable foraging experience, follow these basic safety guidelines:

- Never eat a plant you cannot positively identify.
- Avoid foraging in polluted areas, such as roadsides or contaminated sites.
- Be aware of local regulations and restrictions on harvesting wild plants.
- Exercise caution when foraging in unfamiliar areas, and watch out for hazards such as poisonous plants, stinging insects, and uneven terrain.

Here's a quick tale of one of my foraging adventures recently and a reminder that safety should always be first.

It was a sunny, crisp autumn morning when I embarked on a foraging adventure at Cape Flattery, the northwesternmost point of the contiguous United States. I had heard tales of the rugged beauty and abundant wild edibles that flourished along the rocky coastline, and I couldn't wait to explore this wild, untamed corner of the Pacific Northwest. As I set off on the trail leading me to the cape, I marveled at the towering Sitka spruce trees and the lush, green ferns that carpeted the forest floor. The air was filled with the scent of saltwater and damp earth, and I could feel my excitement growing with each step.

As I ventured deeper into the forest, I spotted a patch of bright, succulent sea lettuce clinging to the rocky shoreline. The emerald-green algae glistened in the sunlight, beckoning me to harvest a handful of its tender, salty fronds. I knew it would make a delicious addition to my foraged feast, so I carefully inched toward the walkway's edge, eager to claim my prize. As I was about to pluck a few fronds, I felt the world shift beneath my feet. My heart skipped a beat as I realized I had stepped on a particularly slick section of the walkway. In that heart-stopping moment, I teetered on the edge of the narrow boardwalk, with nothing but the cold, churning ocean waiting to embrace me below.

With a surge of adrenaline, I instinctively threw my weight backward, desperately trying to regain my balance. My hands scrambled for purchase on the moss-covered railing, but it, too, was slick with dew. Time seemed to slow down as I willed myself not to fall, acutely aware of the unforgiving rocks and pounding waves just a few feet below. Miraculously, I managed to find my footing just in time, narrowly avoiding a terrifying plunge into the ocean's icy depths. My heart raced as I took a few deep, shaky breaths, grateful to have escaped unscathed.

With a newfound respect for the forces of nature and the treacherous beauty of Cape Flattery, I decided to leave the sea lettuce where it was, opting instead to enjoy the stunning views and the exhilarating thrill of having survived my close call. As I returned to the trailhead, I couldn't help but chuckle at the irony of my predicament. Here I was, searching for nourishment in the wild, only to be reminded that Mother Nature is as fierce as she is generous. Ultimately, I returned home empty-handed but filled with a deeper appreciation for the delicate balance between risk and reward and the importance of staying grounded, even when the promise of wild, delicious treasures lures you to the edge.

Embrace the Seasons:

Each season brings its unique array of wild edibles, offering a diverse and ever-changing selection of flavors and textures. By tuning into the cycles of nature, you'll be able to anticipate and appreciate the subtle shifts in the landscape, deepening your connection with the plants and the land.

Gather the Right Tools:

The right tools can make your foraging experience more enjoyable and efficient. Some essential items to consider include the following:

- A sturdy foraging basket or bag
- A reliable field guide
- A pocket knife or pair of scissors for harvesting
- Gloves to protect your hands
- A small notebook to record your finds and observations

Keep it Fun and Engaging:

Foraging is as much a journey of discovery as it is a culinary adventure. Get creative with your wild edibles by trying new recipes, experimenting with different preparation techniques, and sharing your foraged finds with friends and family. The more you immerse yourself in wild foods, the more you uncover the myriad of ways they can enrich your life and nourish your body and soul.

Continue Learning:

As you gain experience and confidence in foraging, you'll find there's always more to learn and explore. Delve deeper into the world of wild edible plants by attending workshops, joining foraging clubs, or connecting with experienced foragers in your community. Expanding your knowledge and skills will help you become a more proficient forager and foster a greater appreciation for the complex relationships between humans and the natural world.

Document Your Foraging Adventures:

Keeping a foraging journal or log can be valuable for tracking your progress and refining your skills. Record your observations, discoveries, and reflections, including details about the plants you've identified, their habitats, and the time of year they were found. Over time, you'll amass a wealth of knowledge and personal insights that can inform and inspire your future foraging endeavors.

Respect the Land and Other Foragers:

As you immerse yourself in the world of foraging, always remember the importance of treating the environment and your fellow foragers with respect and consideration. Practice leave-no-trace principles, avoid trespassing on private property, and be mindful of your actions impact on the landscape and its inhabitants. By fostering a spirit of stewardship and community, we can help ensure that the joys of foraging are accessible to all, now and for future generations.

Armed with this guide to foraging, you're well on your way to unearthing nature's rich culinary treasures. As you venture into the wild, remember to approach your foraging adventures with curiosity, mindfulness, and a deep respect for the earth and its many gifts. By embracing the principles of ethical, sustainable, and responsible foraging, you'll discover not only the incredible flavors and textures of wild edible plants but also forge a lasting connection with the land, the plants, and yourself. Happy foraging!

2 FORAGING WITH A CONSCIENCE
TIPS AND TRICKS FOR ETHICAL AND SUSTAINABLE HARVESTING

Unearthing the bountiful treasures hidden within the verdant landscapes of the Pacific Northwest can be an exhilarating experience, but as we journey through forests and meadows in search of wild edibles, it's crucial to remember the importance of ethical and sustainable foraging. This ensures that we not only protect our natural environment but also preserve its abundance for future generations to enjoy. In this chapter, we'll explore essential tips and tricks that will empower you to forage responsibly while satisfying your adventurous spirit.

Ethical Foraging Tips:

1. *Know Before You Go:*

- *Familiarize yourself with local laws and regulations regarding foraging.*
- *Obtain necessary permits, respect property boundaries, and adhere to collection guidelines.*
- *Be aware of any restrictions that may apply to specific plants or locations.*

2. *Leave No Trace:*

- *Minimize your impact on the environment by avoiding trampling, soil compaction, or damage to surrounding vegetation.*
- *Dispose of waste responsibly and be mindful of your actions in the landscape.*

- *Practice the "Leave No Trace" principles to protect the ecosystem and its inhabitants.*

Sustainable Foraging Tips:

1. Harvest with Abundance in Mind:

- *Focus on collecting species that are plentiful and resilient to the impact of harvesting.*
- *Avoid picking rare, threatened, or endangered plants.*
- *As a general rule, harvest no more than 10-20% of a given population to ensure its continued health and vitality.*

2. Timing and Life Cycle Considerations:

- *Harvest plants at the optimal stage of their life cycle for both nutritional value and minimal impact on the plant's ability to reproduce.*
- *Be mindful of the needs of wildlife that may rely on the plant for food or habitat.*
- *Consider seasonal changes and how they might affect the plant's role in the ecosystem.*

3. Sustainable Harvest Techniques:

- *Use appropriate tools and gentle methods to minimize damage to plants and their surrounding environment.*
- *Employ clean, sharp tools like scissors or pruners to make clean cuts that promote rapid healing and reduce the risk of disease.*
- *When harvesting roots or tubers do so sparingly and selectively to avoid excessive soil disturbance or removal of entire plants.*

Embracing ethical and sustainable foraging practices not only helps protect the beautiful landscapes of the Pacific Northwest but also fosters a deeper connection with the natural world. By following these tips and tricks, you'll be equipped to harvest wild edibles responsibly while cultivating a sense of stewardship and care for the ecosystems that nurture and sustain us. So, grab your foraging basket and set out on a thrilling adventure, secure in the knowledge that you're treading lightly on the earth and contributing to the preservation of our shared wild heritage. Happy foraging!

PART TWO
EXPLORING THE GREAT OUTDOORS
A JOURNEY THROUGH THE STATES OF THE PACIFIC NORTHWEST

3 OREGON
DISCOVER THE ENCHANTING BEAUTY

Venture into the breathtaking landscapes of Oregon, a state that boasts a remarkable variety of terrain, inviting you to explore its stunning natural beauty. From rugged coastlines and lush forests to snow-capped mountains and a high arid desert, each region of Oregon offers a unique and captivating experience. Our journey will take us to well-known areas within Oregon, unveiling the geological wonders that await you in this enchanting Pacific Northwestern paradise.

"To put it simply, Oregon is an inspiration."

-BEVERLY CLEARY, AMERICAN AUTHOR, AND OREGON NATIVE.

Get ready to embrace the ever-changing beauty of Oregon's weather patterns! From cozy, rain-kissed winters to sun-soaked summer days, you'll find each season adds a unique charm to the state's diverse landscapes.

Spring (March-May)

- Mild temperatures averaging between 40°F to 65°F
- Occasional rain showers, especially in the western region
- Blooming wildflowers and blossoming cherry trees

Summer (June-August)

- Warm and sunny, with temperatures ranging from 50°F to 80°F
- Minimal rainfall, making it the ideal season for outdoor activities
- Long days with plenty of daylight hours for exploration

Fall (September-November)

- Crisp, cool temperatures between 35°F and 65°F
- Vibrant foliage in shades of red, orange, and yellow
- Occasional rain and fog, particularly in the western region

Winter (December-February)

- Cold and wet with temperatures ranging from 30°F to 50°F
- Frequent rain and snow in the mountains create a winter wonderland for skiing and snowboarding
- Coastal storms that bring dramatic waves crashing on the shoreline

From rugged coastlines to towering mountains and beyond, let's explore the state's captivating territory and the unforgettable attractions and foraging hotspots that await.

Oregon Coast: A rugged coastline stretching over 360 miles, offering picturesque beaches, dramatic cliffs, and charming coastal towns.

Areas of Interest:

- *Cannon Beach:* Famous for its iconic Haystack Rock, this charming coastal town offers stunning beach views and a vibrant art scene.
- *Cape Perpetua:* A scenic area boasting tide pools, old-growth forests, and breathtaking vistas, such as the Devil's Churn and Thor's Well.
- *Oregon Dunes National Recreation Area:* A unique coastal ecosystem boasting a diverse range of edible plants, including sea rocket, beach pea, and sea kale.

Cascade Range: A mountain range featuring snow-capped peaks, dense forests, and an array of outdoor recreational opportunities.

Areas of Interest:

- *Mount Hood:* A foraging hotspot that boasts Oregon's highest peak at 11,249 feet, offering year-round skiing, hiking trails, and the historic Timberline Lodge. It also has wild edibles such as huckleberries, morels, and chanterelles.

- *Crater Lake National Park:* Home to the deepest lake in the United States, formed by a volcanic eruption, with spectacular views and hiking trails.

Willamette Valley: A fertile valley nestled between the Coast and Cascade Ranges, known for its agriculture, vineyards, and wineries, as well as its abundance of wild greens, berries, and nuts, including miner's lettuce, salal berries, and hazelnuts.

Areas of Interest:

- *Willamette Valley Vineyards:* Taste world-class Pinot Noirs and other wines while enjoying the picturesque vineyard views.
- *Silver Falls State Park:* Explore the "crown jewel" of the Oregon State Parks system, featuring ten stunning waterfalls and miles of hiking trails.

Columbia River Gorge: A dramatic canyon carved by the Columbia River showcasing an array of breathtaking waterfalls, hiking trails, and scenic vistas that offers a wide variety of foraging opportunities, from wild asparagus and nettles to elderberries and blackberries.

Areas of Interest:

- *Multnomah Falls:* The tallest waterfall in Oregon, plunging 620 feet into the Columbia River Gorge, with a historic lodge and picturesque bridge.
- *Hood River:* A haven for outdoor enthusiasts, offering windsurfing, kiteboarding, and access to the scenic Fruit Loop driving tour.

Central Oregon: A high desert region with a diverse landscape, including unique geological formations, volcanic monuments, and scenic rivers.

Areas of Interest:

- *Smith Rock State Park:* A rock-climbing mecca with striking rock formations, miles of hiking trails, and stunning views of the Crooked River.
- *Newberry National Volcanic Monument:* Discover lava flows, cinder cones, and the serene Paulina and East Lakes within this volcanic wonderland.

Eastern Oregon: Vast expanses of high desert featuring otherworldly landscapes, rugged mountains, and fascinating remnants of the state's pioneer past.

Areas of Interest:

- *Painted Hills:* One of the Seven Wonders of Oregon, these colorful hills showcase millions of years of geological history.
- *Wallowa Lake:* A scenic glacial lake surrounded by the majestic Wallowa Mountains, offering outdoor activities such as hiking, fishing, and boating.

Ready to embark on a tasty adventure and connect with nature in a new way? Join one of Oregon's local foraging groups, where you'll uncover the state's hidden culinary treasures while making new friends and learning valuable skills.

• **Oregon Foraging Society:** A community of plant enthusiasts and foragers that hosts events and workshops annually. Website: https://www.oregonforagingsociety.org

• **Wild Food Adventures:** Offers educational workshops, guided tours, and foraging events led by expert John Kallas. Website: https://www.wildfoodadventures.com

• **Portland Urban Foraging Meetup:** A meetup group organizes foraging events, nature walks, and educational gatherings in the Portland area. Website: https://www.meetup.com/Portland-Urban-Foraging-Meetup

• **Cascadia Wild:** A non-profit organization that hosts foraging workshops, plant identification classes, and wilderness skills courses in the Pacific Northwest. Website: https://www.cascadiawild.org

• **Wild Harvest:** Offers plant walks, foraging workshops, and medicinal plant classes in the southern Willamette Valley. Website: https://www.wildharvestoregon.com

As you journey further into the Pacific Northwest, take advantage of the opportunity to explore Oregon's equally enchanting neighbor, Washington State.

4 THE WONDERS OF WASHINGTON
A FORAGER'S PARADISE IN THE EVERGREEN STATE

Welcome to Washington! Embark on an unforgettable journey—a captivating destination known for its diverse landscapes, awe-inspiring natural beauty, and rich cultural heritage. From the lush rainforests of the Olympic Peninsula to the dramatic peaks of the Cascade Range, the serene islands of Puget Sound, to the rolling hills of the Palouse, Washington offers an exciting array of experiences for every type of traveler. Delve into the state's fascinating weather patterns, explore its varied landscape, and connect with local foraging groups as you uncover the wonders of this Pacific Northwestern gem.

"Washington is a place with stunning, generous nature, and a state of mind that is both innovative and open."

- SHERMAN ALEXIE, AMERICAN AUTHOR, AND WASHINGTON NATIVE.

Discover the fascinating and diverse weather patterns that define Washington State's distinct seasons as we guide you through the climate variations experienced throughout the year.

Spring (March to May):

- Mild temperatures are averaging 45-65°F.
- A mix of rain and sunshine

- Spring blooms begin to appear throughout the state.

Summer (June to August):

- Warm and sunny
- Temperatures range from 65-85°F.
- Coastal areas remain cooler, while Eastern Washington can see temperatures above 90°F.

Fall (September to November):

- Cooler temperatures are averaging 50-70°F.
- Rainfall gradually increases, especially in the western regions.
- Crisp air and colorful foliage

Winter (December to February):

- Cold and wet, with temperatures ranging from 30-45°F.
- The western regions experience significant rainfall.
- The eastern regions receive more snow.

As you journey through Washington State, prepare to be awed by its breathtaking scenery. Each region boasts its own distinct character and offers an array of experiences for outdoor enthusiasts, nature lovers, and adventurers alike.

Olympic Peninsula: Home to temperate rainforests, rugged coastline, and the Olympic Mountains, this region boasts unparalleled natural beauty and diverse ecosystems.

Areas of interest:

- Olympic National Park: A UNESCO World Heritage Site, this vast park boasts temperate rainforests, alpine meadows, and stunning coastlines, providing a rich habitat for various wild edibles, such as salal berries, nettles, and chanterelle mushrooms.
- *Hoh Rainforest:* One of the largest temperate rainforests in the US, characterized by moss-covered trees and abundant ferns.
- *Ruby Beach:* A picturesque coastal location with dramatic sea stacks, driftwood, and tide pools teeming with marine life.

Puget Sound: A complex system of waterways, islands, and inlets that create a unique and diverse landscape.

Areas of interest:

- *San Juan Islands:* An archipelago known for its pristine beauty, abundant wildlife, and charming small towns. These islands boast a mild climate and a rich array of wild edibles, including sea vegetables like seaweed and sea lettuce.
- *Whidbey Island:* The largest island in Puget Sound, featuring scenic vistas, quaint seaside villages, and Fort Casey State Park.
- *Deception Pass State Park:* A popular park encompassing rugged cliffs, forested trails, and stunning views of the Deception Pass Bridge and surrounding waters.

Cascade Range: A mountain range that stretches from southern British Columbia to Northern California, featuring some of the most iconic peaks in Washington.

Places to visit include:

- *Mount Rainier:* The highest peak in Washington, a glaciated stratovolcano and the centerpiece of Mount Rainier National Park. This park features lush old-growth forests, subalpine meadows, and a diverse array of wild edibles, including huckleberries, wild ginger, and morels.
- *Mount St. Helens:* An active stratovolcano that famously erupted in 1980, now a popular destination for hiking and outdoor recreation.
- *North Cascades National Park:* A vast wilderness area encompassing jagged peaks, deep valleys, and numerous glaciers.

Eastern Washington: A region characterized by a diverse landscape of rolling hills, arid shrub-steppe, and striking geological formations.

Places to visit include:

- *Channeled Scablands:* Unique geological features created by massive Ice Age floods, featuring deep coulees, basalt cliffs, and the stunning Dry Falls cataract.
- *Columbia River Gorge:* A deep canyon carved by the Columbia River, marking the border between Washington and Oregon and offering a wealth of recreational opportunities.
- *Dry Falls:* Once the site of the world's largest waterfall, this striking cataract offers sweeping views of the surrounding coulee and basalt cliffs.

Southwest Washington: A region rich in history, natural beauty, and recreational opportunities, including the Columbia River and the Lewis River Valley.

Places to visit include:

- *Mount St. Helens National Volcanic Monument:* A protected area surrounding the volcano, offering opportunities for hiking, wildlife viewing, and learning about the eruption's impact.
- *Gifford Pinchot National Forest:* A sprawling forest encompassing diverse ecosystems, including old-growth forests, meadows, and alpine lakes, and offers prime foraging opportunities for wild berries, mushrooms, and medicinal plants, such as yarrow and elderberries.
- *Vancouver:* A historic city along the Columbia River, offering cultural attractions, parks, and easy access to nearby natural areas.
- *Cape Disappointment State Park:* Featuring picturesque lighthouses, stunning coastal views, and rich maritime history, this park is a must-visit destination for nature lovers.

Ready to explore Washington's wild bounty and connect with fellow nature enthusiasts? Dive into our list of local foraging groups. You'll find guided tours, workshops, and community gatherings designed to help you unearth the delicious and nutritious edibles hidden in the Evergreen State's diverse landscapes.

- **Washington Foragers Association:** A community dedicated to ethically and sustainably harvesting wild plants and fungi, offering events and workshops throughout the year. Website: https://www.waforagers.com
- **Foraged and Found Edibles:** A company specializing in wild food and mushroom foraging, offering workshops, guided tours, and foraged products. Website: https://www.foragedandfoundedibles.com
- **Seattle Urban Foraging Meetup:** A meetup group organizing foraging events, nature walks, and educational gatherings in the Seattle area. Website: https://www.meetup.com/Seattle-Urban-Foraging-Meetup
- **The Wilderness Awareness School:** A non-profit organization that hosts foraging workshops, plant identification classes, and wilderness skills courses in Washington. Website: https://www.wildernessawareness.org

As you venture beyond the Pacific Northwest, you'll discover that the United States is brimming with an abundance of edible plants, offering foraging opportunities from coast to coast. From the succulent berries of New England's forests to the nutritious greens of the Southwest's deserts, the nation's diverse ecosystems provide a treasure trove of flavors and culinary possibilities. In the next chapter, "Feast from the Wild," we'll introduce you to some of the most widespread and easily identifiable wild edibles nationwide. So, join us as we embark on a compelling journey through America's wild pantry, uncovering the delicious and nutritious plants that await in our backyards.

PART THREE
NATURE'S PANTRY
A GUIDE TO COMMON WILD EDIBLE PLANTS

Alfalfa
Medicago sativa [MEH-DIH-KOH-GO SUH-TY-VUH]

In the 1850s, Chilean seed producers imported alfalfa to California. This perennial flowering plant belongs to the Fabaceae (legume) family. Common names include Lucerne, Chilean Clover, Buffalo Herb, California Clover, Purple Medic, Spanish Clover, Trefoil, Holy Hay, and Barseem.

Locate: Though widely grown as a forage crop for livestock, there are some cases where alfalfa may be found growing wild, such as in disturbed areas or along roadsides.

Identification:

GROWTH/SIZE - A perennial herb that can grow up to 3 feet tall.

BARK/STEM/ROOT - The stem is upright, smooth, and branched, with a diameter of approximately 0.2 inches. The root system is well-developed, with a taproot reaching 10-20 feet deep.

Leaf - The leaves are compound, dark green, and have smooth surfaces with serrated edges, three leaflets that are ovate to elliptical, measuring approximately 0.5-1 inch long and 0.2-0.6 inches wide.

Flower - The flowers are small with a distinctive clover-like shape. They are arranged in clusters on the stem, with a bright purple color. The flower clusters are generally 2-4 inches long and can produce numerous seed pods.

Fruit/seed/nut - The fruit is a typically oblong pod containing several tiny, round seeds.

Look-a-like(s): *Sweet Clover* (*Melilotus species*) is a common roadside plant that resembles alfalfa. It has yellow or white flowers that grow in spikes and three-parted leaves. *White Clover* (*Trifolium repens*) is a common lawn plant that resembles alfalfa. It has white or pink flowers that grow in round clusters and three-parted leaves.

Caution: Alfalfa seed products may cause reactions similar to the autoimmune disease called lupus erythematous. Alfalfa might also cause some people's skin to become extra sensitive to the sun. Wear sunblock outside, especially if you are light-skinned.

Culinary Preparation: Alfalfa flowers from June to July, and the seeds ripen from July to September. Raw alfalfa leaves, and sprouts have a slightly nutty and mild flavor and can be consumed raw. Healthy and flavorful, they are often used in sandwiches, smoothies, and juices. The sprouts are highly nutritious and low in calories, making them a popular choice for health-conscious consumers.

Medicinal Properties: Alfalfa is a rich source of vitamins, minerals, and antioxidants and has been used as a nutritional supplement to support overall health and well-being. Some traditional medicinal uses of alfalfa include relieving indigestion, bloating, and gas. Some modern therapeutic use studies have shown that it has prebiotic effects, which means it can help promote the growth of beneficial gut bacteria. It also has wound-healing properties and may help treat skin conditions such as psoriasis and eczema.

Fun Fact: The name "alfalfa" is derived from the Arabic word "al-fasfasah," which means "father of all foods." This name reflects the plant's reputation as a highly nutritious forage crop.

Dog Toxicity: It's generally considered safe for dogs when consumed in small amounts. Its often used as a dietary supplement and can be found in many commercial pet foods.

Allegheny Blackberry
Rubus alleghemiensis [ROO-BUS AL-LEH-GAY-NEE-EN-SIS]

The Allegheny Blackberry is a part of the Rosaceae (rose) family. They are found throughout North America. Blackberry bush growth is increased after a natural disaster such as a fire but will die back after the tree seedlings it protects start to take root and grow.

Locate: You can find blackberries at the edges of wooded areas, gardens, wastelands, along roadways, and at the edges of fields and meadows.

Identification:

GROWTH / SIZE - Blackberry bushes are easy to spot. Here are a few tidbits that should help if you aren't sure. A deciduous, native shrub that grows in a tangle of canes up to 8 ft tall and 10 feet wide.

BARK/STEM/ROOT - These stems are brown or reddish brown with stout prickles that are straight or slightly curved. The tips are green where there's new growth.

Leaf -There are usually three or *palmately compound* leaves with long *petioles*. Each leaflet is up to 4" long and 3" wide; they're generally twice as long as broad. There are usually two serrated margins on an *ovate* leaflet. The leaves will change to Red, orange, or purple in the fall before dropping their leaves for winter.

Flower - Five-petaled white flowers appear in loose terminal clusters from May to June. *Racemes* of about 12 white flowers appear on the canes. No floral scent is present.

Fruit/seed/nut - July is fruit season. Depending on moisture levels, *aggregate drupes* are around 3/4" long and 1/3" wide in the summer. Initially, the *drupes* are white or green, then red, then black. They're seedy and sweet when fully ripened. The fruit should come off the stem clean, revealing a solid, fleshy core.

Look-a-like(s): They can sometimes be mistaken for black raspberries, which are also edible. Several other members of the Rubus genus are similar as well.

Cautions: Take care when harvesting blackberries, and wear long sleeves; the thorns can be nasty.

Culinary Preparation: You can eat blackberries raw as you are harvesting or with a sprinkling of sugar once home for a tad of extra sweetness. They also work very well when baked into a pie or turned into jam.

Medicinal Properties: The roots are anti-hemorrhoidal, anti-rheumatic, astringent, stimulant, and tonic. An infusion can treat stomach complaints, diarrhea, piles, coughs and colds, tuberculosis, and rheumatism. The infusion has also been used by women threatened with a miscarriage. Infusions of the root can be used to soothe sore eyes. The leaves are astringent. An infusion can be used in the treatment of diarrhea. Urinary problems have been treated with an infusion of the bark. A decoction of the stems has been used as a diuretic.

Fun Fact: In the UK, some believe blackberries should not be harvested after October 11th (Old Michaelmas Day). They think that after this day, the devil will spit, step or foul the berries, making them unfit to eat. Because October is cool, humid, and often wet, a bacteria called Botryotinia can invade the berries, causing them to go rancid and causing illness.

Dog Toxicity: Not toxic to your furry friends.

Black Elderberry

Sambucus canadensis [SAM-BOO-kus KAN-AH-DEN-SIS]

There are two types of elderberries in the Mid-Atlantic region. The most common is the black elderberry. Still, you can find red elderberries in some parts of the state. It is a member of the Adoxaceae (muskroot) family. Common names are American Elder, American Elderberry, and Common Elderberry.

Locate: Elderberries like moist soil. You can find them along roadsides, trails, fences, and forests. They also grow in swamps and wasteland.

Identification:

GROWTH / SIZE - This tree is native to North America and is a woody, *deciduous* shrub or small tree that grows from 5 to 12 feet tall and 6 to 10 feet wide.

BARK/STEM/ROOT - Short *lenticels* on the bark give it a warty appearance. The bark is yellowish gray to light grayish brown. A young woody branch has scattered *lenticels* that are light grayish brown. Shoots are pale green when young, and the *pith* is white.

LEAF - The leaves are bright green and have 5 to 11 leaflets, but most have 7. They are *oval* to *lance-shaped*, measuring 2 to 6 inches long and 0.5 to 2.5 inches wide. There's a wedge-shaped base with an abruptly narrow tip. In the fall, the foliage turns yellow.

FLOWER - During June, creamy-white fragrant flowers with six petals shaped like a star appear in flat-topped or rounded clusters between 4 and 10 inches.

FRUIT /SEED/NUT - There are clusters of rounded, edible, purple-black *drupes*. The berries measure 1/4 inch across, have 3-5 seeds, and are in bulky clusters.

Look-a-like(s): *Pokeweed* (*phytolacca americana*), a plant that produces larger berries that hang in a long cylinder, and the *Devil's Walking Stick* (*Aralia spinosa*); berries are similar in appearance to elderberries, but the main stem has large thorns.

Caution: Remember that elder stems, leaves, and unripe berries are toxic and should not be consumed. Only the flowers and ripe berries are edible; the berries need to be cooked before eating. All parts of the plant contain *cyanogenic glycosides*, which are metabolized into cyanide when consumed. Cooking helps destroy the compound, making them harmless. Some mild symptoms include nausea, vomiting, and diarrhea. Elderberries can lead to coma and death if not prepared properly.

Culinary Preparation: Elderflowers can be used to make cordial or wine. The berries make a great addition to fruit pies, jams, or jellies.

Medicinal Properties: This berry is helpful for colds, touches of flu, and H1N1 "swine" flu. Additionally, it boosts your immune system and is used for HIV/AIDS. You can also use elderberry for sinus pain, back and leg pain (sciatica), nerve pain (neuropathy), and chronic fatigue syndrome (CFS).

Besides treating hay fever (allergic rhinitis) and cancer, elderberries are used as laxatives, diuretics, and sweat inducers. It can also be used to combat heart disease, high cholesterol, headaches, toothaches, and weight loss.

Fun Fact: These plants can self-pollinate, but flies are their primary pollination source.

Dog Toxicity: the leaves, stems, unripe fruit, and root are poisonous to dogs as they contain cyanide, even if only in small quantities.

Chickweed
Stellaria media [STELL-AR-EE-UH MEED-EE-UH]

Chickweed grows everywhere, which is excellent news for foragers because it's almost as tasty as it is nutritious. It's also effortless to harvest. It's part of the Caryophyllaceae (carnation) family and has multiple names, such as starweed, Birdweed, Chickenwort, Starweed, Starwort, Winterweed, and mouse ear.

Locate: Chickweed grows almost everywhere, including backyards, parks, grasslands, fields, and wastelands.

Identification: Common chickweed is an annual in colder climates but becomes evergreen and perennial in warmer ones. It is best suited for temps between 53°F and 68°F.

GROWTH / SIZE - It grows in large patches, forming mats that can grow to 1-2 feet tall and round.

BARK/STEM/ROOT - The succulent stems are green or burgundy and often have white hairs.

Leaf - The leaves are oval-ovate, broadly elliptic along their margins, hairless on top, and occasionally hairy on the bottom. The stems at the bottom of the plant have short, hairy petioles, while the leaves near the tip are sessile. They are more prominent at the ends of the stems, spanning up to ¾ inch in length and ½ inch across.

Flower - There are white, small flowers with distinctly lobed petals. In most cases, there are three stamens and three styles. The flowers don't take long to form capsules; a plant can have both flowers and capsules.

Fruit/seed /nut - Seed capsules replace each flower; they're light brown, with six small teeth along their upper rim and several seeds. Mature seeds are reddish brown, slightly flattened, and orbicular-reniform; they have minute bumps on their surface.

Look-a-like(s): One toxic look-alike is the scarlet pimpernel. You can tell the difference by looking for the line of fine hairs along the stem, as the scarlet pimpernel doesn't have it. The flowers are also reddish-orange, and the plant itself has milky sap.

Caution: Nausea, upset stomach, diarrhea, and vomiting can result from too much chickweed.

Culinary Preparation: You can eat chickweed raw in salads or use it to make pestos or green smoothies. Chickweed will keep in the fridge for a few days if you wrap it in a damp paper towel and put it in a plastic bag. It also freezes reasonably well if you blend it up first.

Medicinal Properties: Soothing, cooling, hydrating, and healing, chickweed has it all for skin inflammation, wounds, boils, rashes, acne, and drawing out infections. It's applied topically as a plant poultice or infused in olive oil. Our ability to absorb nutrients improves when we eat chickweed. Combining this with the high fiber and mineral content makes chickweed a highly effective digestive support aid.

Fun Fact: Chickweed makes excellent food for poultry as well.

Dog Toxicity: Chickweed is not toxic for dogs; quite the opposite. There are several uses for chickweed when it comes to your best friend.

- **Hotspots and Skin irritation:** make a poultice using chickweed to soothe burns, hotspots, and skin irritations.
- **Tinctures:** used as an astringent to help clean and heal minor skin wounds by applying juice fresh from the stem.
- **Tea:** because it's tasty and easy for pups to digest, it can be used to soothe the occasional upset stomach.

Chicory
Cichorium intybus [SIK-KOR-EE-UM IN-TYE-BUS]

Chicory is incredibly common, and once you know what to look for, you'll probably find it everywhere. It belongs to the Asteraceae (daisy) family. It is known by several names, such as blue daisy, blue dandelion, blue sailors, blueweed, coffee weed, cornflower, horseweed, and wild endive.

Locate: Chicory grows readily in disturbed areas, like wastelands, meadows, fields, and roadsides.

Identification:

GROWTH /SIZE - You can spot chicory by looking for distinctive blueish-purple flowers. This biennial plant grows from two to four feet tall and one foot wide.

BARK/STEM/ROOT - It has erect green or reddish-brown stems with a fleshy taproot that exudes a milky sap when cut.

Leaf - Generally, alternate leaves are up to eight inches long and two inches wide, becoming smaller as they ascend the stem. These leaves are lance-shaped and resemble dandelion leaves at the base. The leaves gradually narrow where they are sessile or clasp the stem. Depending on where the leaves are on the stem, they have lobed edges, dentate edges, or they lose their petioles and hold the stem. In the lower leaf surface, the central vein usually has many hairs.

Flower - With numerous bright blue rays and blunt-toothed edges, these flowers have ligulate flower heads up to 1.5 inches long. These flowers have no stalks and grow along stems, opening up in the morning and closing up by noon unless it's cloudy, appearing from mid-summer until the first frost.

Fruit/seed/nut - Has achene with a brown oval shape, five ribs, and blunt ends. On the broader end, there are bristles across the top.

Look-a-like(s): Chicory plants are distinctive with their flowers and have no toxic relatives. Among wildflowers, only dandelions and daisies are easily identifiable for a beginner forager.

Caution: Chicory might have been sprayed with herbicides as it's considered a weed. Avoid harvesting chicory that's too close to busy roads.

Culinary Preparation: The leaves and flowers are bitter and can be used in salads. Use sparingly and, if need be, blanch the leaves to take away some of the bitterness. In addition, chicory roots can also be roasted, ground, or blended with coffee to make a less expensive and caffeine-free beverage.

Medicinal Properties: In the laboratory, root extracts have also been shown to be antibacterial, anti-inflammatory, and mildly sedative. In addition, they slow down and weaken the pulse, as well as lower blood sugar levels. Extracts from leaves have similar effects, though they are weaker. To treat swellings, bruised leaves were used as a poultice. A root extract can treat fevers and jaundice, as well as as a diuretic and laxative.

Fun Fact: Initially brought to the United States by the colonists as a medicinal herb, chicory was cultivated by Thomas Jefferson and others as a forage crop. As it does not dry well, horses, cattle, sheep, poultry, and rabbits were usually fed green.

Dog Toxicity: Chicory is pet safe and can benefit your pet's health.

Dandelion
Taraxacum officinale [TA-RAKS-UH-KUM OH-FISS-IH-NAH-LEE]

Dandelions are one of the most common edibles and are found all over the world. They're easy to spot, which makes them a fantastic foraging option for beginners. They belong to the Asteraceae (daisy) family and have only one different name: Lion's tooth.

Locate: Dandelions prefer shady, cooler areas, but you'll also find them in direct sunlight. To the distaste of many homeowners, they grow on lawns. Potential habitats include parks, pastures, orchards, hayfields, meadows, and disturbed areas such as roadsides and wastelands.

Identification:

GROWTH/SIZE - You can quickly identify Dandelions by their distinctive yellow blooms. It is a fast-spreading broadleaf perennial weed that spreads by seed. The plant grows 2-6 inches tall and can get as wide as 2 feet.

BARK/STEM/ROOT - Leafless and unbranched hollow stems form deep taproots, and milky latex sap flows throughout the plant.

Leaf - A basal rosette is formed in an oblanceolate shape. Deeply toothed, backward-pointing teeth or lobes are present on rosette leaves at the base.

Flower - A bright yellow ray flower with toothed tips appears throughout the year on second-year plants. In the evening, they close their petals, single heads on their stems.

Fruit/seed/nut - Seed heads are fluffy, round, downy, and dispersed by the wind.

Look-a-like(s): *Cat's Ear* (*Hypochaeris radicata*) is the most likely to be mistaken for a dandelion, as the flower heads look very similar. Cat's Ear does not have hollow stems, and their stems are branching. They also have hairy leaves with deep notches. *Sow Thistle* (*Sonchus spp.*) also does not have hollow stems, and the leaves grow up the entire stalk with multiple flowers growing from each branch. In the thistle family, the mature plant also has prickly spines.

Caution: No plant-related, but check if they have been sprayed with a weed killer before eating.

Culinary Preparation: The entire dandelion plant is edible, but you must prepare the greens and the root differently. The greens can be eaten raw or added to salads, they have an earthy and bitter taste, and it's best to use young leaves. The leaves can also be sautéed in olive oil and garlic and seasoned. Flowers can make dandelion wine, syrups, or even baked like zucchini blossoms. Chopping and roasting the roots can be used to create tea.

Medicinal Properties: The dandelion is a commonly used herbal remedy. It is especially effective and valuable as a diuretic because it contains high potassium salts and can replace the potassium lost from the body when used. The plant is used internally to treat gall bladder and urinary disorders, gallstones, jaundice, cirrhosis, dyspepsia with constipation, edema associated with high blood pressure and heart weakness, chronic joint and skin complaints, gout, eczema, and acne. The latex contained in the plant sap can be used to remove corn, warts, and verrucae.

Fun Fact: The yellow flowers can be dried and ground into a yellow-pigmented powder and used as a dye.

Dog Toxicity: Dandelion, though not toxic, can cause constipation and gas in some dogs. Your pup can eat the whole plant if you find a fresh patch. The dandelion will boost its immune system and help improve digestion. It also aids in building strong bones and teeth.

Dog Rose
Rosa canina [ROH-SUH KUH-NYE-NUH]

Roses aren't just beautiful. Some roses produce fruits called rosehips. Rosehips are the bulbous area under the flower itself. They are called the fruit of the rose and come in striking colors such as red to orange, and you can even find black or yellow varieties. They are easily found in the wild and belong to the Rosaceae (rose) family. Other common names are Brier Hip, Dog Brier, Dog Rose Fruit, Hip Berries, Witches Brier, and Hip Rose. Several types of roses produce rosehips. Check out these varieties for your best shot at finding your prize. Dog Rose (Rosa canina), Rugosa Rose (Rosa rugosa), Prickly Wild Rose (Rosa acicularis), and Cinnamon Rose (Rosa cinnamomea).

Locate: Roses are an excellent beginner forage; they are well-known and easily spotted. Wild roses can be found in fields, scrub, and disturbed areas along roadsides, hiking trails, and woodland edges.

Identification:

GROWTH / SIZE - the plant is a shrub and grows rapidly to a height of 9 feet.

BARK/STEM/ROOT - this shrub has very sharp, stout, curving thorns.

LEAF - There are 5–7 leaflets on its pinnate leaves with teeth lining the edge of the leaf blade. When bruised, the leaves smell amazing. As the weather gets colder, the leaves drop.

FLOWER - The flowers are usually pale pink but can also be deep pink or white. They bloom from June to July. Each flower has five petals and measures approximately 1.6-2.4 inches. When the sepals are viewed from underneath, two are whiskered (or bearded) on both sides, two are smooth, and one has a whisker (or beard) on just one side.

FRUIT/SEED/NUT - the rosehips ripen from October to December and tend to be sweeter after the first frost.

Look-a-like(s): Several wild rose species can be found while foraging. Wild strawberries, hawthorn, and crab apple are other wildflowers in the rose family. Briars, brambles, raspberries, and cloudberries are all close relatives you will likely find on your journey.

Caution: As with other thorny plants, avoid getting injured while harvesting the fruit. Below the fruit's flesh is a layer of hair around the seeds. If you eat them, they can irritate your mouth and digestive tract.

Culinary Preparation: The wild dog rose is considered the best rosehip source. Rosehips can be made into syrup as a great way to add more vitamin C to your diet. You can make jams, jellies, and pies or use them to make tea or wine.

Medicinal Properties: They're a brilliant source of vitamin C, up to 20 times more than oranges. Rosehips contain Lycopene and carotene, like carrots. Therefore, it makes sense that they would benefit the skin and eyes.

Fun Fact: Rosehips have gained plenty of notoriety in the beauty and healthcare industries for several reasons. Let's start with the beauty industry; Rosehip oil has been used for years to delay the signs of aging, though there is little scientific proof.

Dog Toxicity: You don't have to worry about your dog getting sick from roses. Their flowers, petals, and rose hips are non-toxic.

Purslane
Portulaca oleracea [POR-TEW-*LAK*-UH AWL-LUR-*RAY*-SEE-UH]

Purslane is another weed that's common throughout North America. It is a part of the Portulacaceae (purslane) family. It goes by these other names: Garden Purslane, Little Hogweed, Moss Rose, Pigweed, Portulaca, Red Root, Rock Moss, Verdolaga, and Wild Portulaca.

Locate: Purslane grows in wastelands and disturbed areas, such as gravelly soil and cracks in the sidewalk.

Identification:

GROWTH/SIZE - It's a low-growing, succulent annual plant that can grow up to 8 inches in height and 18 inches in width.

BARK/STEM /ROOT - The stem is fleshy and reddish-green, with a prostrate growth habit that produces many lateral branches. The roots are fibrous and shallow.

Leaf - The leaves are small, oval-shaped, ranging from 0.5 to 1.5 inches long. They are fleshy and succulent and range in color from green to red. The leaves grow alternately along the stem and have a smooth surface.

Flower - The flowers are small and cup-shaped, measuring approximately 0.5 to 0.75 inches in diameter. They are typically yellow but also pink, white, or red. The flowers bloom in the summer months and are produced in the axils of the leaves.

Fruit/seed/nut - The fruit is a small capsule that contains many tiny, black seeds. The seeds are approximately 0.05 inches in diameter and are dispersed by wind and water. The plant also reproduces by rooting at the nodes of the stem, allowing it to spread rapidly and form dense mats on the ground.

Look-a-like(s): As mentioned before, spurges are the closest toxic look-alike to Purslane. The easiest way to tell the difference is to look for fleshy, succulent leaves. Spurges have flatter leaves and exude white latex when broken.

Caution: It may interact with certain medications and cause digestive upset or allergic reactions.

Culinary Preparation: Immerse your collected Purslane in water to eliminate seeds and dirt. Get rid of thick stems and store them in the refrigerator. It has a mild, lemony flavor with a nice crunch. You can eat it raw in salads and sandwiches or steam it as a side dish. It also makes a delicious soup.

Medicinal Properties: It has been used for medicinal purposes for centuries in traditional Ayurveda, Chinese, and Unani cultures. Some traditional medicinal uses: anti-inflammatory properties due to the presence of flavonoids. It improves digestion and relieves constipation. Treats wounds, burns, and skin infections. It treats respiratory ailments such as asthma, coughs, and bronchitis. Its also used in modern medicine for its potential health benefits. Here are some of the modern medicinal uses: studies have shown it may have anti-cancer effects, potentially due to its high antioxidant content and ability to inhibit cancer cell growth.

Fun Fact: It was a popular food among ancient Greeks and Romans, who believed it to have medicinal properties and ate it as a vegetable. The plant was also a common food source among Native Americans, who used it to make porridge or boil it as a green vegetable.

Dog Toxicity: Purslane is toxic to your pup and can cause a metabolic imbalance. Some signs of metabolic imbalance are hypersalivation, weakness, and tremors. If your dog exhibits these symptoms, it could be at risk for kidney failure.

PART FOUR
NATURE'S SWEET TREASURES
WILD FRUITS AND BERRIES

Scan for full color photos

Black Hawthorn
Crataegus douglasii [KRUH-TEE-GUS DUHG-LAS-EE-EYE]

The Black Hawthorn has been an essential resource for Indigenous peoples in its native regions. They utilized the plant for food, medicine, and tools, making it a versatile and valuable asset. Today, the Black Hawthorn continues to captivate interest as an ornamental plant for its various applications in traditional and modern medicine.

Location: A native shrub or small tree found in the Pacific Northwest. It thrives in various habitats, including forests, meadows, stream banks, and rocky slopes.

Identification:

GROWTH/SIZE: Grows to a height of 10-30 feet, with a spread of 8-20 feet. It has a slow to moderate growth rate and can develop a dense, thicket-forming habit, providing excellent habitat for wildlife.

BARK/STEM/ROOT: The bark is dark gray to blackish-brown, becoming fissured and scaly with age. The stems have sharp, stout thorns growing up to 1.5 inches long. The root system is fibrous and shallow, allowing the plant to tolerate various soil types.

Leaf: The leaves are simple, alternate, and lobed, measuring 1-3 inches long and 1-1.5 inches wide. They are dark green on the upper surface and paler green below.

Flower: It produces clusters of small, white flowers in late spring. These flowers are 5-petaled and have a sweet, musky scent that attracts pollinators.

Fruit/Seed/Nut: The fruit is a small, dark purple to black pome, resembling a tiny apple. It measures about 0.3-0.5 inches in diameter and contains a few hard seeds. The fruit ripens in late summer to early fall and is an important food source for wildlife.

Look-a-like(s): Some non-toxic look-a-likes include other species of hawthorns and serviceberries. A poisonous look-a-like is the European spindle (*Euonymus europaeus*). Both species have relatively small, simple leaves arranged oppositely or alternately along the stem, depending on the species. The leaf shapes are similar, with ovate or elliptical forms and serrated edges.

Cautions: none known

Culinary Preparation: Black Hawthorn fruits can be used in various culinary preparations. They are often processed into jellies, jams, syrups, and wines. The fruit's astringent taste can be mellowed by cooking or blending with sweeter fruits.

Medicinal Properties: Traditionally, Indigenous peoples have used Black Hawthorn for treating various ailments, including digestive issues, heart problems, and skin conditions. Modern research has shown that hawthorn extracts contain bioactive compounds with antioxidant, anti-inflammatory, and cardioprotective properties. Some studies suggest that hawthorn extracts may help lower blood pressure, improve heart function, and reduce symptoms of heart failure.

Fun Fact: During the Victorian era, Black Hawthorn was believed to bring bad luck if brought inside the home. This superstition likely arose from the association of Hawthorn with ancient burial sites and the belief that it was a "fairy tree" inhabited by spirits.

Dog Toxicity: Black Hawthorn fruits are generally considered non-toxic to dogs. Be cautious of the thorns, as they can cause injuries to curious dogs exploring the plant.

Blackcap Raspberry
Rubus leucodermis [ROO-BUS LOO-KO-DER-MIS]

The Blackcap Raspberry, also known as Whitebark Raspberry or Blue Raspberry, belongs to the Rosaceae (rose) family and is a beloved plant with a colorful history. It has been highly valued for its flavorful and nutritious fruit. Indigenous people have utilized the plant as a food source and for medicinal purposes, while European settlers admired its taste and versatility in various culinary applications.

Location: This deciduous shrub is native to western North America, from Alaska to California and stretching eastward to the Rocky Mountains. It can be found in habitats such as open woodlands, meadows, and along forest edges.

Identification:

GROWTH/SIZE: It typically grows 3-6 feet tall, forming dense thickets through its spreading root system. The plant has a moderate growth rate and provides excellent cover for wildlife.

Bark/Stem/Root: The bark is a distinguishing characteristic, as it has a whitish, waxy coating, giving it the name "Whitebark Raspberry." The stems are covered in fine prickles and become brownish-gray as they mature. The extensive root system can form new shoots, allowing the plant to spread and colonize an area.

Leaf: The leaves are palmately compound, usually with three to five leaflets. They are dark green and somewhat wrinkled on the upper surface, while the undersides are paler and covered in fine hairs.

Flower: The flowers are small, white, and five-petaled, appearing in clusters from late spring to early summer. The flowers attract pollinators, such as bees and butterflies, which help with fruit production.

Fruit/Seed/Nut: The fruit is a small, dark purple to black drupelet that resembles a typical raspberry. It ripens in mid to late summer and is a favorite food source for wildlife, including birds and mammals.

Look-a-like(s): There are no known toxic look-a-likes, but some non-toxic look-a-likes include other species of raspberries and blackberries.

Cautions: None known.

Culinary Preparation: Blackcap Raspberries are delicious as jams, jellies, pies, and sauces. They can also be eaten fresh, added to salads or desserts, or even used as a topping for yogurt or ice cream. The possibilities are endless.

Medicinal Properties: Traditionally, Indigenous peoples have used various parts of the plant to treat ailments such as wounds, diarrhea, and stomach issues. Modern research on raspberries suggests that they contain antioxidants and other beneficial compounds.

Fun Fact: The Blackcap Raspberry's botanical name, Rubus leucodermis, is derived from the Greek words "leuco," meaning white, and "dermis," meaning skin, which refers to the plant's characteristic white bark.

Dog Toxicity: The fruit is generally considered safe for dogs. As a precaution, it is advisable to prevent dogs from ingesting large amounts of the plant, especially the leaves or stems, which may cause gastrointestinal upset.

Blue Elderberry
Sambucus caerulea [SAM-*BYOO*-KUS SEH-*REW*-LEE-UH]

The Blue Elderberry is a captivating plant with an intriguing history. Belonging to the Adoxaceae (moschatel) family, this deciduous shrub or small tree has been utilized by various cultures for centuries for its edible fruits and medicinal properties. Other common names for Blue Elderberry include Blueberry Elder, Mexican Elder, and Blue Elder.

Location: It's native to western North America, from Oregon to Baja, California, and eastward to west Texas. It thrives in habitats like open woodlands, riparian areas, canyons, and chaparral environments, often growing at elevations between 200-3,300 meters.

Identification:

GROWTH/SIZE: Typically grows 10-30 feet tall with a rounded, somewhat irregular crown. It has a moderate to fast growth rate and can form dense thickets, providing excellent cover and habitat for wildlife.

BARK/STEM/ROOT: The bark is thin, with shallow furrows and ridges, and has a grayish-brown color. The branches are stout, with a smooth, light grayish-brown outer surface. The root system is fibrous and shallow, allowing the plant to tolerate various soil types.

Leaf: The leaves are pinnately compound, usually with 5-9 leaflets, each measuring 2-6 inches long and 1-2 inches wide. The leaflets are elliptical to lance-shaped, with serrated margins, a dark green color on the upper surface, and a paler shade of green underneath.

Flower: It produces large, flat-topped clusters of small, white to creamy flowers in late spring to early summer. The flowers are fragrant and attract pollinators, such as bees and butterflies.

Fruit/Seed/Nut: The fruit is a small, round drupe that ripens to a dark blue or purple-black color with a whitish, waxy bloom. The fruits are typically ripe in late summer to early fall and are an essential food source for various bird species and other wildlife.

Look-a-like(s): Non-toxic look-a-likes include the American Elderberry and Red Elderberry.

Cautions: It is essential to cook the berries before consumption, as the raw fruit contains mildly toxic compounds that heat neutralizes. The plant's leaves, stems, and roots contain harmful compounds and should not be ingested.

Culinary Preparation: The ripe berries can be used in various culinary preparations, such as jams, jellies, syrups, pies, and wines.

Medicinal Properties: Traditionally, various parts of the Blue Elderberry plant have been used by Indigenous peoples to treat ailments like colds, fever, and rheumatism. Modern research suggests that elderberries contain bioactive compounds with antioxidant, antiviral, and anti-inflammatory properties. Some studies have shown that elderberry extracts may help reduce the severity and duration of cold and flu symptoms.

Fun Fact: The Blue Elderberry has been used by various Indigenous tribes to create musical instruments, such as flutes and clapper sticks, due to the plant's lightweight and easily hollowed-out stems. This highlights the cultural significance of the plant beyond its culinary and medicinal uses.

Dog Toxicity: It is advisable to prevent dogs from ingesting the plant, especially the leaves, stems, and unripe fruits, which contain toxic compounds.

Indian Plum
Oemleria cerasiformis [OHM-LAIR-EE-UH SEH-RUH-SIH-FORM-ISS]

The Indian Plum belongs to the Rosaceae (rose) family. This deciduous shrub is known by other common names such as Osoberry, Oregon Plum, and Skunkbush. Indigenous peoples have traditionally used various parts of the Indian Plum for food, medicine, and cultural practices.

Location: Indian Plum is native to the Pacific coast, from British Columbia to central California. It can be found in various habitats, including moist woodlands, stream banks, and forest edges, where it often grows as an understory plant.

Identification:

GROWTH/SIZE: It typically grows between 6-16 feet tall, forming dense thickets. It is often one of the first shrubs to leaf out and flower in the spring, providing an early nectar source for pollinators.

Bark/Stem/Root: The bark is thin, smooth, and reddish-brown. The branches are slender, with a greenish-brown hue. The root system is fibrous, allowing the plant to tolerate various soil types and moisture levels.

Leaf: The leaves are simple, lance-shaped, and measure 2-5 inches long. The upper surface of the leaves is shiny and dark green, while the underside is paler and slightly hairy. In the spring, the young leaves can have a mild cucumber-like fragrance.

Flower: It produces small, greenish-white, fragrant flowers in early spring before the leaves emerge. The flowers appear in drooping clusters, with male and female flowers usually on separate plants (dioecious).

Fruit/Seed/Nut: The fruit is a small, oblong drupe measuring 1-2.5 cm long. It ripens to a bluish-black in mid to late summer and is a crucial food source for wildlife, including birds and mammals.

Look-a-like(s): There are no known toxic look-alikes for the Indian Plum. However, some non-toxic look-alikes include Salmonberry (*Rubus spectabilis*) and Thimbleberry (*Rubus parviflorus*), which we will explore later.

Cautions: none known.

Culinary Preparation: The fruit can be eaten fresh, although the taste is somewhat astringent. They can make jams, jellies, and sauces or be added to various desserts. The young leaves can also be used as a tea substitute.

Medicinal Properties: Traditionally, it's been used to treat ailments such as colds, sore throats, and digestive issues. Modern research on the medicinal properties of the Indian Plum is limited, so I won't list any here.

Fun Fact: The Indian Plum's early blooming flowers provide an essential early source of nectar for pollinators, such as bees and hummingbirds, making it a valuable plant for supporting biodiversity in its native habitats.

Dog Toxicity: They have not been known to cause any toxicity in pups, but like with anything else, moderation is key.

Ocean Spray
Holodiscus discolor [HOH-LUH-DIS-KUS DIH-SKUH-LUHR]

The Ocean Spray also belongs to the Rosaceae (rose) family. This deciduous shrub is known by other common names such as Creambush, Ironwood, and Foamflower. Its delicate, cascading clusters of flowers have earned it the charming nickname "Ocean Spray," as they resemble sea spray when in full bloom.

Location: Ocean Spray is native to the western parts of North America, from southern Alaska to California and eastward to the Rocky Mountains. It can be found in various habitats, including open woodlands, chaparral, and along forest edges or rocky slopes, where it often grows as an understory plant.

Identification:

GROWTH/SIZE: Ocean Spray typically grows between 3-15 feet tall, forming dense thickets with arching branches. It has a moderate growth rate and provides excellent cover for wildlife.

Bark/Stem/Root: The bark is thin, reddish-brown to gray, and becomes fissured and scaly as the plant matures. The branches are stout, with a grayish-brown color and a rough texture. The root system is fibrous, allowing the plant to tolerate various soil types and moisture levels.

Leaf: The leaves are simple, alternate, and measure 1-3 inches long. They are broadly ovate to heart-shaped, with toothed margins, and are dark green on the upper surface, while the undersides are paler and covered in fine hairs.

Flower: It produces long, arching clusters of small, creamy-white flowers in late spring to early summer. The flowers are fragrant and attract pollinators, such as bees and butterflies.

Fruit/Seed/Nut: The fruit is a small, dry, brown achene that persists on the plant throughout the winter. The fruits provide a food source for various bird species and other wildlife.

Look-a-like(s): There are no known toxic look-alikes. Some non-toxic look-alikes include Bridal Wreath Spirea (*Spiraea prunifolia*) and Meadowsweet (*Filipendula ulmaria*). Proper identification is essential to ensure safe consumption and use.

Cautions: While Ocean Spray is not commonly used for culinary purposes, the flowers can make a fragrant tea or as an attractive garnish.

Culinary Preparation: None Known.

Medicinal Properties: Traditionally, Indigenous peoples have used various parts of the Ocean Spray plant to treat ailments such as skin irritations, eye infections, and digestive issues.

Fun Fact: Ocean Spray's rugged and durable wood has been used by Indigenous peoples for making tools, such as digging sticks and spear shafts, highlighting the plant's importance in traditional cultures beyond its aesthetic appeal.

Dog Toxicity: unable to find any information on the toxicity to your pup, so I would avoid it just to be safe.

Oregon Cherry
Prunus emarginata [PROO-NUHS EE-MAR-JUH-NEY-TUH]

The Oregon Cherry belongs to the Rosaceae (rose) family. Familiar names like Bitter Cherry and Wild Cherry also know this deciduous tree or shrub.

Location: Oregon Cherry is native to the western parts of North America, from Alaska to California. It can be found in various habitats, including moist woodlands, stream banks, and forest edges, where it often grows as an understory plant.

Identification:

GROWTH/SIZE: It typically grows between 15-50 feet tall, depending on the conditions. It has a rounded crown and spreading branches, providing a picturesque appearance.

BARK/STEM/ROOT: The bark is thin and smooth, reddish-brown to gray. As the tree matures, the bark may become fissured and scaly. The branches are slender and reddish-brown, with an alternating leaf arrangement. The root system is fibrous, allowing the plant to tolerate various soil types and moisture levels.

LEAF: The leaves are simple, elliptical, and measure 1-3 inches long. They have finely toothed margins and a dark green color on the upper surface, while the undersides are paler and slightly hairy.

FLOWER: It produces small, white to pinkish, fragrant flowers in clusters in early spring. The flowers attract a variety of pollinators, such as bees and butterflies.

FRUIT/SEED/NUT: The fruit is a small, round drupe measuring about 1/2 inch in diameter. It ripens to a bright red color in mid to late summer and is an essential food source for wildlife, including birds and mammals.

Look-a-like(s): There are no known toxic look-a-likes for the Oregon Cherry. Some non-toxic look-a-likes include Chokecherry (*Prunus virginiana*) and Pin Cherry (*Prunus pensylvanica*).

Cautions: Most, if not all, members of this genus produce hydrogen cyanide, a poison that gives almonds their flavor. You can taste the bitter taste of this toxin in the leaves and seeds. In small amounts, it's not harmful, but bitter seeds or fruits shouldn't be eaten.

Culinary Preparation: The fruit can be eaten fresh, although the taste can be quite bitter. They are commonly used to make jams, jellies, and syrups or added to various desserts. The tree's inner bark can be dried and ground into a flour substitute.

Medicinal Properties: Traditionally, various parts of the Oregon Cherry plant have been used to treat ailments such as colds, coughs, and digestive issues.

Fun Fact: The wood of the Oregon Cherry is prized for its reddish-brown color and fine grain, making it a popular choice for creating decorative woodwork and small objects, such as tool handles and musical instruments.

Dog Toxicity: The seeds, leaves, and stems of the Oregon Cherry contain cyanogenic glycosides, which can be toxic to dogs if ingested in large amounts. Poisoning symptoms may include vomiting, excessive drooling, difficulty breathing, seizures, and death.

Oregon Grape

Mahonia aquifolium [MUH-HOH-NEE-UH UH-KWIF-OH-LEE-UHM]

The Oregon Grape belongs to the Berberidaceae (barberry) family. This evergreen shrub is known by other common names such as Holly-leaved Barberry, Mountain Grape, and Oregon Holly Grape. Oregon Grape has a rich history of use by Indigenous peoples for food, medicine, and dye.

Location: Oregon Grape is native to western North America, from southern British Columbia to northern California. It can be found in various habitats, including coniferous forests, mixed woodlands, and open areas, where dense thickets often form.

Identification:

GROWTH/SIZE: It typically grows between 3-6 feet tall, with an upright, spreading habit. It has a slow to moderate growth rate providing excellent ground cover and wildlife habitat.

Bark/Stem/Root: The bark is thin, grayish-brown, and has a rough texture. The branches are stout and often exhibit a reddish hue. The root system is shallow and spreading, with bright yellow underground rhizomes.

Leaf: The leaves are pinnately compound, with 5-9 spiny, holly-like leaflets. They are glossy, dark green on the upper surface and have a paler, matte finish on the underside.

Flower: It produces small, bright yellow flower clusters in early to mid-spring. The flowers are fragrant and attract pollinators, such as bees and butterflies.

Fruit/Seed/Nut: The fruit is a small, round, bluish-black berry with a waxy bloom, ripening in late summer.

Look-a-like(s): Oregon Grape has no known toxic look-a-likes. Some non-toxic look-a-likes include Leatherleaf Mahonia (*Mahonia bealei*) and Creeping Mahonia (*Mahonia repens*), both of which are a part of the same plant family.

Cautions: The plant's leaves are prickly and can cause skin irritation. It contains a compound called berberine. Berberine can interact with certain medications, and high doses may cause gastrointestinal discomfort, such as cramping or diarrhea.

Culinary Preparation: Oregon Grape berries can make jams, jellies, and syrups or be added to various desserts. The berries taste tart, so they are often combined with sweeter fruits. The bright yellow roots can be used as a natural dye.

Medicinal Properties: Traditionally, various parts were used, particularly the roots, to treat ailments such as skin infections, digestive issues, and fever. Modern research has confirmed the presence of the alkaloid berberine, which possesses antimicrobial, anti-inflammatory, and liver-protective properties.

Fun Fact: Oregon Grape was designated as the state flower of Oregon in 1899, reflecting its significance and beauty within the region.

Dog Toxicity: It's not considered highly toxic to dogs but could potentially cause gastrointestinal upset in dogs, such as vomiting or diarrhea.

Nootka Rose
Rosa nutkana [ROH-SUH NUT-KAH-NUH]

The Nootka Rose is a member of the Rosaceae (rose) family. Known for its beauty and utility, this wild rose species also goes by the names Nutka Rose and Wild Rose. The Nootka Rose has been appreciated for centuries for its ornamental value and its use in various traditional applications.

Location: It thrives along the Pacific Coast from Alaska to California. It can be found in various habitats such as meadows, open forests, stream banks, and coastal dunes, where it often forms dense thickets and provides shelter for wildlife.

Identification:

GROWTH/SIZE: A deciduous shrub typically grows between 3-10 feet tall. It has an upright, spreading habit, with arching stems that create an appealing appearance.

BARK/STEM/ROOT: The bark is grayish-brown, while the stems are green to reddish and covered with straight, stout prickles. The root system is fibrous and spreading, enabling the plant to form dense thickets and tolerate various soil types and moisture levels.

LEAF: the leaves are pinnately compound, with 5-7 oval leaflets with serrated edges. They are a bright green, turning yellow in the fall before dropping.

FLOWER: It produces showy, pink flowers 2-3 inches wide in late spring to early summer. The flowers have a sweet fragrance, attracting a variety of pollinators, including bees and butterflies.

FRUIT/SEED/NUT: The fruit is a small, round, red-to-orange "hip" that ripens in late summer or early fall. The hips are an important food source for birds and other wildlife.

Look-a-like(s): Nootka Rose has no known toxic look-a-likes. Some non-toxic look-a-likes include the Wood's Rose (*Rosa woodsii*) and the Baldhip Rose (*Rosa gymnocarpa*).

Cautions: Like other members of the rose family, it has thorns on its stems, which can cause injury or skin irritation.

Culinary Preparation: Nootka Rose hips can make jams, jellies, syrups, and teas. They are rich in vitamin C and can be eaten fresh, although they are often processed to remove the seeds and hairs before consumption.

Medicinal Properties: Traditionally, Indigenous peoples have used various parts of the Nootka Rose plant, particularly the hips, to treat ailments such as digestive issues, colds, and sore throats.

Fun Fact: Nootka Rose is named after Nootka Sound, a region on the west coast of Vancouver Island, where European botanists first described the plant in the 19th century.

Dog Toxicity: There is no evidence that Nootka Rose is toxic to dogs. If you suspect your dog has consumed Nootka Rose, monitor them for symptoms such as vomiting, diarrhea, or lethargy.

Red Huckleberry
Vaccinium parvifolium [VUH-SIN-EE-UM PAR-VI-FOH-LEE-UM]

Red Huckleberry is a delightful plant known for its flavorful berries and ornamental appeal. A member of the Ericaceae (heather or heath) family, the Red Huckleberry is also called Small-leaved Huckleberry and Red Bilberry.

Location: It ranges from Alaska to central California. It can be found in various habitats, including coniferous forests, mixed woodlands, and open areas. Red Huckleberry often grows on decaying wood, stumps, and logs, indicating its preference for nutrient-rich, acidic soils.

Identification:

GROWTH/SIZE: A deciduous shrub typically grows between 3-10 feet tall. It has a slender, upright growth habit with arching branches.

BARK/STEM/ROOT: The bark is smooth and reddish-brown. The stems are slender, green to red, and covered with fine hairs. The shallow and fibrous root system allows the plant to thrive in nutrient-poor soils.

Leaf: the leaves are small, oval, and alternately arranged on the stems. They are green to yellowish-green with finely toothed margins.

Flower: It produces tiny, bell-shaped, pinkish-white flowers in spring. The flowers are often hidden beneath the leaves and attract various pollinators, including bees and hummingbirds.

Fruit/Seed/Nut: The fruit is a small, bright red berry with a sweet-tart taste. The berries ripen in mid to late summer and are an essential food source for birds and other wildlife.

Look-a-like(s): There are no known toxic look-a-likes for Red Huckleberry. Some non-toxic look-a-likes include the Evergreen Huckleberry (*Vaccinium ovatum*) and Blue Huckleberry (*Vaccinium deliciosum*).

Cautions:

Culinary Preparation: Red Huckleberries can be eaten fresh but are often used in jams, jellies, pies, and muffins. They can also be dried or frozen for later use.

Medicinal Properties: Traditionally, Indigenous peoples have used Red Huckleberry leaves and bark for medicinal purposes, such as treating pain, inflammation, and digestive issues. Modern research on the medicinal properties of Red Huckleberry is limited. However, berries are rich in vitamin C, antioxidants, and other nutrients.

Fun Fact: In many Indigenous cultures, Red Huckleberry has been an essential food source, and gathering these berries has been a communal activity that brings families and communities together.

Dog Toxicity: Red Huckleberry is not toxic to your pup.

Salal
Gaultheria shallon [GAWL-THEER-EE-UH SHUH-LOHN]

Salal is an evergreen shrub with a wide range of uses. Belonging to the Ericaceae (heather or heath) family, Salal is also known as Shallon and Lemonleaf. This versatile plant has been utilized for its edible berries, medicinal properties, and ornamental value by Indigenous peoples and early settlers.

Location: Salal is native to the western regions of North America, from Alaska to California. It can be found in various habitats, including coastal forests, open meadows, and rocky bluffs. Salal thrives in well-drained, acidic soils and is commonly found growing in the understory of coniferous forests.

Identification:

GROWTH/SIZE: Salal is an evergreen shrub that grows tall between 3-15 feet tall. It has a dense, spreading growth habit, forming thickets and providing excellent ground cover.

BARK/STEM/ROOT: The bark is reddish-brown and peeling. The stems are slender, green to reddish, and often hairy. The shallow and fibrous root system allows the plant to colonize and stabilize soils in its native habitats.

LEAF: Salal leaves are thick, leathery, and dark green with a shiny upper surface. They are oval to lance-shaped, have finely serrated edges, and measure 1.5-4 inches long.

FLOWER: It produces clusters of small, bell-shaped, pinkish-white flowers in late spring to early summer.

FRUIT/SEED/NUT: The fruit is a small, dark purple to black berry with a sweet, mild flavor. The berries ripen in late summer to early fall.

Look-a-like(s): There are no known toxic look-a-likes for Salal. Some non-toxic look-a-likes include the Evergreen Huckleberry (*Vaccinium ovatum*) and Kinnikinnick (*Arctostaphylos uva-ursi*).

Cautions: as with any plants, some may experience an allergic reaction to Salal. If you experience any signs of an allergic reaction, such as skin rash, difficulty breathing, or swelling, discontinue use and seek medical attention.

Culinary Preparation: Salal berries can be eaten fresh or used in jams, jellies, and pies and made into fruit leather. The berries have a mild, sweet flavor and are high in vitamin C and antioxidants.

Medicinal Properties: Traditionally, Indigenous peoples have used various parts of the Salal plant, particularly the leaves, and berries, for medicinal purposes. They have been used to treat digestive issues, wounds, and inflammation.

Fun Fact: Indigenous peoples have used Salal leaves for various purposes, including as a natural food preservative. The leaves were often placed in dried fish or meat containers to keep them fresh.

Dog Toxicity: No evidence suggests that Salal is toxic to dogs.

Salmonberry
Rubus spectabilis [ROO-BUHS SPEK-TAB-UH-LIS]

Salmonberry is a beautiful and delicious plant cherished for its vibrant flowers and flavorful berries. Salmonberry is also called Raspberry Bush and Cloudberry and belongs to the Rosaceae (rose) family.

Location: Salmonberry is native to the western coastal regions of North America, from Alaska down to northern California. It can be found in various habitats, including moist forests, stream banks, and coastal bluffs. Salmonberry thrives in damp, fertile soils and is commonly found in the understory of temperate rainforests.

Identification:

GROWTH/SIZE: Salmonberry is a deciduous shrub typically growing between 3-13 feet tall. It has an erect to spreading growth habit, with arching, thorny branches.

Bark/Stem/Root: The bark is brown to grayish, while the stems are reddish to purple with scattered prickles. The root system comprises rhizomes that allow the plant to spread and form dense thickets.

Leaf: The leaves are bright green, compound, and typically have three toothed leaflets. They are alternately arranged on the stems, and the leaflets have pointed tips and serrated edges.

Flower: It produces large, showy flowers in spring, usually in shades of pink to magenta. The flowers have five petals and are 1-2 inches in diameter.

Fruit/Seed/Nut: The fruit is a juicy, orange-to-red berry that resembles a raspberry. The berries ripen in late spring to early summer.

Look-a-like(s): There are no known toxic look-alikes for Salmonberry. Some non-toxic look-alikes include the Thimbleberry (*Rubus parviflorus*) and the Red Raspberry (*Rubus idaeus*). Proper identification is essential to ensure safe consumption and use.

Cautions: none known.

Culinary Preparation: Salmonberries can be eaten fresh or used in jams, jellies, pies, and smoothies. The berries have a sweet, tart flavor and are rich in vitamin C and antioxidants.

Medicinal Properties: Traditionally, Indigenous peoples have used various parts of the Salmonberry plant, particularly the berries and young shoots, for medicinal purposes. They have been used to treat digestive issues and soothe sore throats.

Fun Fact: Salmonberry has been an essential food source for Indigenous peoples, and its harvesting often coincides with the arrival of salmon runs, which is how the plant got its name.

Dog Toxicity: They are not toxic to dogs.

Spreading Gooseberry
Ribes divaricatum [RYE-BEEZ DYE-VUH-RY-KAH-TUM]

Spreading Gooseberry is a resilient plant known for its spiny stems and delicious berries. A Grossulariaceae (currant) family member, Spreading Gooseberry, is also called Straggly Gooseberry and Coast Black Gooseberry.

Location: Spreading Gooseberry is native to the western coastal regions of North America, from Alaska to central California. It can be found in various habitats, including moist forests, stream banks, and coastal bluffs. Spreading Gooseberry thrives in damp, well-drained soils and is commonly found in the understory of temperate rainforests.

Identification:

GROWTH/SIZE: A deciduous shrub typically grows between 3-6 feet tall. It has a sprawling growth habit, with arching, thorny branches that spread out from the base.

Bark/Stem/Root: The bark is grayish-brown, while the stems are reddish to green, covered with spines and bristles. The root system is fibrous, enabling the plant to establish itself in various soil conditions.

Leaf: The leaves are bright green, palmately lobed, and have a rounded shape. They are alternately arranged on the stems and have serrated edges.

Flower: It produces small, pendulous flowers in spring, usually in shades of greenish-white to pink. The tubular flowers attract pollinators, such as bees and hummingbirds.

Fruit/Seed/Nut: The fruit of Spreading Gooseberry is a small, dark purple to black berry that has a sweet, slightly tart flavor. The berries ripen in summer.

Look-a-like(s): There are no known toxic look-alikes for Spreading Gooseberry. Some non-toxic look-alikes include the Black Currant (Ribes nigrum) and the Red Currant (Ribes rubrum).

Cautions: none known.

Culinary Preparation: The fruit can be eaten fresh or used in jams, jellies, pies, and sauces. The berries have a sweet, slightly tart flavor and are rich in vitamin C and antioxidants.

Medicinal Properties: Traditionally, Indigenous peoples have used various parts of the Spreading Gooseberry plant, particularly the berries, for medicinal purposes. They have been used to treat digestive issues, fever, and inflammation.

Fun Fact: Indigenous peoples have also used the spiny stems of Spreading Gooseberry to make fish traps and as a natural barrier to protect food caches from predators.

Dog Toxicity: There is no evidence to suggest that Spreading Gooseberry is toxic to dogs.

Snowberry
Symphoricarpos albus [SIM-FOR-IH-KAR-POHS AL-BUHS]

Snowberry is a small deciduous shrub that belongs to the Caprifoliaceae (honeysuckle) family. This plant is valued for its ornamental qualities and distinctive white berries. Other common names for Snowberry include Waxberry, Ghostberry, and White Coralberry.

Location: Snowberry can be found throughout North America, from Alaska to northern Mexico. It is particularly prevalent in the Pacific Northwest and the northern Rocky Mountains. This plant thrives in many habitats, including forests, meadows, and riparian zones. Snowberry prefers well-drained soils and can be found in full sun to partial shade.

Identification:

GROWTH/SIZE: Snowberry is a small to medium-sized shrub, typically growing 3-6 feet tall. Its dense and rounded growth habit makes it an excellent choice for hedges and borders.

Bark/Stem/Root: The bark is smooth and grayish-brown, while the stems are slender and reddish-brown. The root system is shallow and fibrous, allowing the plant to spread and form dense thickets.

Leaf: The leaves are simple, opposite, and oval-shaped with smooth edges. They are generally dark green on the upper surface and lighter green on the lower surface.

Flower: It produces small, bell-shaped flowers in clusters during late spring to early summer. The flowers are pinkish-white.

Fruit/Seed/Nut: The most distinctive feature of Snowberry is its fruit: small, round, white berries that persist through winter. Although the berries are not palatable for humans, they provide a valuable food source for birds and small mammals.

Look-a-like(s): There are no toxic look-alikes for Snowberry.

Cautions: Snowberry is considered mildly toxic to humans due to saponins in the berries. Consuming large quantities of berries may cause gastrointestinal distress, so it is best to avoid ingesting them.

Culinary Preparation: Snowberry is not typically used in culinary preparations due to its unpalatable taste and mild toxicity.

Medicinal Properties: Native Americans used Snowberry for various medicinal purposes, including treating skin conditions, fever, and respiratory ailments because of the saponins it contains. The saponins can be toxic but cleanse and heal the skin when applied externally. They kill body parasites and help heal wounds. Sore eyes can be treated with an infusion of the fruit. Chewed leaves have been used as poultices or infusions to treat external injuries.

Fun Fact: Native Americans also used Snowberry branches to make brooms and brushes and for constructing arrow shafts.

Dog Toxicity: Snowberry may be mildly toxic to dogs if consumed in large quantities. Symptoms of ingestion can include vomiting, diarrhea, and abdominal pain.

Thimbleberry

Rubus parviflorus [ROO-BUHS PAR-VI-FLOR-us]

Thimbleberry is a member of the Rosaceae (rose) family. This plant is cherished for its lovely flowers, attractive foliage, and edible berries. Thimbleberry is also known by other common names, such as Western Thimbleberry and Salmonberry, although it should not be confused with Rubus spectabilis, also known as Salmonberry.

Location: Thimbleberry is native to western North America, from Alaska to northern Mexico, with a particular prevalence in the Pacific Northwest and the Rocky Mountain regions. It thrives in various habitats, including moist woodlands, forest edges, and meadows. Thimbleberry prefers well-drained soils and can be found in full sun to partial shade.

Identification:

GROWTH/SIZE: It's a relatively small shrub growing 3-6 feet tall. Its growth habit is erect and spreading, with a tendency to form dense thickets.

Bark/Stem/Root: The bark is smooth, reddish-brown, and peels away in thin strips as it ages. The stems are slender and unarmed, lacking thorns, distinguishing them from many other Rubus species.

Leaf: It has large, maple-like leaves that are simple, alternate, and lobed. The leaves have serrated edges and are bright green on the upper surface, with a lighter green and somewhat hairy lower surface.

Flower: It produces large, white, five-petaled flowers in late spring to early summer. The flowers are about 2 inches wide and are pollinated by various insects.

Fruit/Seed/Nut: Its fruit is a red, raspberry-like drupelet aggregate that matures mid to late summer. The berries are soft, juicy, and easily detach from the receptacle, giving them a thimble-like appearance.

Look-a-like(s): Thimbleberry's non-toxic look-alike is the Salmonberry (*Rubus spectabilis*), which has similar leaves and growth habits, but its berries are orange to red, and the stems have small prickles.

Cautions: none known

Culinary Preparation: Thimbleberry is prized for its sweet, tangy, and mildly tart flavor. The berries can be eaten fresh, used in jams, jellies, and pies, or added to yogurt and smoothies. Due to their delicate nature, Thimbleberries are not commonly found in commercial markets, making them a special treat for those who forage.

Medicinal Properties: Native Americans utilized Thimbleberry for various medicinal purposes, including treating wounds, burns, and digestive issues. Some modern herbalists use Thimbleberry leaves to make a poultice for skin ailments.

Fun Fact: Thimbleberry leaves were used by Native Americans and early settlers as a natural toilet paper due to their large size, soft texture, and availability in the wilderness.

Dog Toxicity: Thimbleberry is not considered toxic to dogs. If your dog consumes Thimbleberry and exhibits symptoms such as vomiting, diarrhea, or lethargy, consult your veterinarian for guidance.

PART FIVE
GREENS GALORE
DISCOVERING NUTRITIOUS AND TASTY WILD GREENS

Scan for full color photos

American Bistort
Polygonum bistortoides [PUH-LIG-OH-NUM BYE-STOR-TOY-DEEZ]

American Bistort, also known as Western Bistort or Smokeweed, is a perennial herb that belongs to the Polygonaceae (knotweed) family. This plant has been historically valued for both its culinary and medicinal properties.

Location: American Bistort is native to western North America, primarily in the western United States and western Canada. It thrives in various habitats, such as meadows, grasslands, and moist subalpine or alpine regions. It typically grows at higher elevations, from 4,000 to 13,000 feet.

Identification:

GROWTH/SIZE: A small herbaceous plant typically grows tall between 8 and 20 inches.

BARK/STEM/ROOT: The plant has a stout, fleshy rhizome that gives rise to a single, erect stem. The stem is slender, green or reddish, and smooth or slightly hairy.

Leaf: It has basal leaves that form a rosette. The leaves are lance-shaped to narrowly elliptic, with smooth edges and a prominent central vein. The leaves are typically 2-6 inches long and have a short, slender petiole.

Flower: The flowers appear in dense, spike-like clusters at the top of the stem. They are small, white, or pinkish and bloom from late spring to early summer.

Fruit/Seed/Nut: The fruit is a small, dark brown, triangular achene that contains a single seed.

Look-a-like(s): It may be confused with Knotweeds (Polygonum spp.), also belonging to the Polygonaceae family. However, Knotweeds have more slender, elongated inflorescences and alternate leaves, while American Bistort has a dense, spike-like inflorescence and basal leaves.

Cautions: none known.

Culinary Preparation: The roots, typically boiling or roasting, can be consumed after cooking. They have a starchy, somewhat sweet flavor and were used by Native Americans as a food source. The young leaves can also be eaten raw or cooked in salads or as a pot herb.

Medicinal Properties: Historically, Native Americans used American Bistort to treat various ailments, such as digestive issues, wounds, and infections. While limited scientific evidence supports these uses, the plant remains popular in traditional medicine.

Fun Fact: The name "Smokeweed" comes from the plant's historical use by Native Americans, who would dry and burn the leaves to create a smoke believed to have medicinal properties.

Dog Toxicity: There is no known toxicity of American Bistort to dogs.

Beach Pea
Lathyrus japonicus [LA-THY-rus juh-PON-ih-kus]

Beach Pea is a perennial flowering plant that belongs to the Fabaceae (legume) family, which includes peas, beans, and other legumes. Beach Pea is also known as Sea Pea, Sea Vetchling, or Circumpolar Pea.

Location: Beach Pea is found in coastal regions of the Northern Hemisphere, including North America, Europe, and Asia. It grows mainly along sandy or gravelly beaches, dunes, and coastal grasslands. Beach Pea prefers well-drained soils and is often found in areas with moderate to high salinity.

Identification:

GROWTH/SIZE: It's a low-growing, trailing, or climbing plant that reaches heights of 4 to 20 inches. It has a sprawling growth habit and may form dense mats.

BARK/STEM/ROOT: The plant has smooth, slender, green, or reddish stems, either prostrate or climbing. Beach Pea's deep taproot system helps it survive in nutrient-poor, sandy soils.

Leaf: The leaves are pinnate, with 4-12 pairs of leaflets and a branched tendril at the tip. Each leaflet is oval or elliptic, measuring about 1-3 cm long. The leaf edges are smooth, and the leaf surface is often shiny.

Flower: It produces showy flowers that are typically purple, violet, or blue, although white and pink varieties also exist. The flowers, measuring about 1/2 to 1 inch across, grow in clusters of 2 to 7 from the leaf axils. The flowering period is from June to September.

Fruit/Seed/Nut: It produces a straight or slightly curved, 1 to 2.4 inches long seedpod. Each pod contains 3 to 8 round or slightly flattened seeds, which are brown to black when mature.

Look-a-like(s): It may be confused with other legume species, such as Common Vetch (*Vicia sativa*), which has pinnate leaves and purple flowers. However, Common Vetch has a more slender and climbing growth habit, and its flowers are more elongated.

Cautions: While Beach Pea seeds are edible in small quantities, they should not be consumed in large amounts due to the presence of a neurotoxic amino acid, L-α-aminooxy-β-phenyl propionic acid (AOPP), which can cause a condition called lathyrism if ingested in high quantities.

Culinary Preparation: The young pods, seeds, and shoots can be eaten either raw or cooked. The seeds can be used as a substitute for common peas, while the young shoots can be added to salads or used as cooked vegetables.

Medicinal Properties: Historically, Beach Pea has been used in traditional medicine to treat digestive issues and as a diuretic. However, there is limited scientific evidence to support these claims.

Fun Fact: Beach Pea is believed to have been an essential food source for early explorers and sailors, who would harvest the plant for its seeds during long sea voyages.

Dog Toxicity: There is no known toxicity to dogs.

Field Horsetail

Equisetum arvense [EH-KWUH-SET-UM AR-VEN-SEE]

Field Horsetail belongs to the Equisetaceae (horsetail) family. This ancient, primitive plant has other common names, including Common Horsetail, Mare's Tail, and Bottlebrush.

Location: Field Horsetail can be found in many environments, including wetlands, meadows, forests, and even disturbed areas like roadsides. It is native to the Northern Hemisphere, including North America, Europe, and Asia.

Identification:

GROWTH/SIZE: Field Horsetail typically grows 8-20 inches tall, although it can occasionally reach 1 meter.

BARK/STEM/ROOT: It has hollow, jointed stems with a silica-rich, rough texture. Stems are green and ribbed, with a central cavity. Field Horsetail has an extensive root system and reproduces through spores and underground rhizomes.

LEAF: Instead of leaves, Field Horsetail has thin, green, needle-like branches that grow from the stem joints, forming a whorl pattern around the stem.

FLOWER: It does not produce flowers. Instead, it produces cone-like structures called strobili at the tips of fertile, non-branching stems.

FRUIT/SEED/NUT: This plant reproduces through spores released from the strobili.

Look-a-like(s): Mare's Tail (*Hippuris vulgaris*): This aquatic plant is sometimes confused with Equisetum species due to its similar, whorled arrangement of leaves. However, unlike horsetails, Mare's Tail has solid stems and does not have the joint structure characteristic of the Equisetum genus. This plant is not considered toxic. Clubmosses (Lycopodiaceae family) are primitive plants that may resemble horsetails due to their growth habit and similar foliage. However, clubmosses have small, needle-like leaves and do not have the jointed stem structure of horsetails. Most clubmoss species are non-toxic but have different uses and properties than horsetails.

Cautions: Although Field Horsetail is non-toxic, it can become a nuisance in gardens and landscapes due to its aggressive growth and difficulty to eradicate.

Culinary Preparation: Young Field Horsetail shoots can be eaten raw or cooked, often used as a wild asparagus substitute. However, only consume Field Horsetail in moderation, as it contains high levels of silica and other compounds that could be harmful in large quantities.

Medicinal Properties: Field Horsetail has a long history of traditional medicinal uses, including as a diuretic, an astringent, and a remedy for kidney and urinary tract issues. Some modern herbalists also use it for skin, hair, and nail health due to its high silica content.

Fun Fact: Field Horsetail is a living fossil dating back over 300 million years. Its ancestors were massive tree-like plants that formed significant components of ancient forests during the Carboniferous period.

Dog Toxicity: There is limited information on the toxicity of Field Horsetail in dogs. While it is generally considered non-toxic, ingesting large amounts could cause gastrointestinal upset.

Fireweed

Chamerion angustifolium [KUH-MEER-EE-ON AN-GUHS-TUH-FOH-LEE-UHM]

Fireweed belongs to the Onagraceae (evening primrose) family. This colorful, resilient wildflower has other common names, including Willowherb, Rosebay Willowherb, and Blooming Sally.

Location: It can be found in various environments, such as open meadows, forests, and disturbed areas like burn sites and landslides. Native to North America, it thrives in temperate and boreal regions.

Identification:

GROWTH/SIZE: A perennial herbaceous plant can grow up to 1.6-8.2 feet tall.

BARK/STEM/ROOT: The plant has a single, erect, and unbranched reddish stem covered in fine hairs.

LEAF: The leaves are long, narrow, and pointed, arranged in an alternate pattern on the stem. They are dark green, with a smooth surface and prominent veins.

FLOWER: The vibrant, showy flowers are magenta or pink and form in tall, spike-like clusters at the top of the stem.

Fruit/Seed/Nut: It produces elongated seed pods that split open when mature, releasing numerous tiny seeds with white, feathery hairs that aid in wind dispersal.

Look-a-like(s): Can be confused with other species like Epilobium or Epilobium-like plants with similar flower colors and shapes. However, these plants are generally non-toxic and do not pose a significant risk if misidentified.

Cautions: There are no significant cautions associated with Fireweed, as it is non-toxic and generally considered safe to consume.

Culinary Preparation: Young Fireweed leaves, and shoots can be eaten raw or cooked and are often used as a potherb. The flowers are edible and can be used as a garnish, while the leaves are sometimes used to make tea.

Medicinal Properties: Traditionally, Fireweed has been used by indigenous peoples to treat inflammation, burns, and skin irritations. It has also been used as a mild sedative, an astringent, and a remedy for gastrointestinal issues.

Fun Fact: Fireweed earned its name due to its remarkable ability to rapidly colonize areas affected by fire or other disturbances, making it one of the first plants to appear after such events.

Dog Toxicity: Fireweed is considered non-toxic to dogs.

Licorice Root
Glycyrrhiza lepidota [GLAHY-SIR-IH-ZUH LEP-IH-DOH-TUH]

Licorice root comes from the Glycyrrhiza glabra, which belongs to the Fabaceae (legume) family. It is also known by other common names, such as Sweet Root, Liquorice, and Gan Zao, in traditional Chinese medicine.

Location: Licorice root can be found in well-draining soils near rivers and streams.

Identification:

GROWTH/SIZE: A perennial herbaceous plant growing 3-5 feet tall.

BARK/STEM/ROOT: The stem is erect and branching, while its most notable feature is the long, fibrous root system that contains the highly prized Licorice root.

LEAF: Licorice leaves are pinnately compound, consisting of 9-17 leaflets arranged alternately. They are green and ovate-lanceolate in shape.

FLOWER: The flowers are small, tubular, and pale blue to violet. They grow in spike-like clusters called racemes.

FRUIT/SEED/NUT: Licorice produces flat, brown, bean-like pods that contain several seeds.

Look-a-like(s): A look-a-like plant is the Licorice (*Glycyrrhiza glabra*), native to Eurasia. It is also non-toxic.

Cautions: It should be consumed in moderation, as excessive intake can lead to side effects such as high blood pressure, water retention, and potassium deficiency.

Culinary Preparation: It's often used as a natural sweetener and flavoring agent in various confectioneries, beverages, and desserts. It can be chewed on raw, steeped as tea, or added to other dishes to impart its distinctive sweet taste.

Medicinal Properties: Traditionally, Licorice root has been used for its anti-inflammatory, expectorant, and demulcent properties. It has been employed to treat conditions such as coughs, colds, ulcers, and digestive issues. Modern research has also shown that Licorice root has potent antiviral and antimicrobial effects.

Fun Fact: Licorice root has been used for over 4,000 years in various traditional medicine systems, making it one of the oldest herbal remedies known to humanity.

Dog Toxicity: Licorice root is considered safe for dogs in small quantities. However, excessive consumption can lead to the same side effects as in humans, such as high blood pressure and potassium deficiency.

Orange Honeysuckle
Lonicera ciliosa [LUH-NISS-ER-UH SIH-LEE-OH-SUH]

The Orange Honeysuckle is a member of the Caprifoliaceae (honeysuckle) family. Other common names, such as Western Trumpet Honeysuckle or Wild Honeysuckle, also know it.

Location: Orange Honeysuckle can be found in the western regions of the United States, from southern Alaska down to California. It grows in various habitats, including forests, woodlands, and riparian areas, and is often found climbing trees or shrubs.

Identification:

GROWTH/SIZE: A deciduous, woody, twining vine growing up to 20 feet long.

BARK/STEM/ROOT: The bark is reddish-brown, while its stems are slender and flexible.

LEAF: The leaves are opposite, simple, and ovate to an elliptic shape. They are dark green on the upper surface and lighter green on the underside.

FLOWER: This plant is known for its vibrant, trumpet-shaped, orange to reddish-orange flowers. The flowers appear in clusters at the ends of branches and are very fragrant.

FRUIT/SEED/NUT: It produces small, inedible, red, or orange berries that contain a few seeds.

Look-a-like(s): A non-toxic look-a-like plant is the Trumpet Honeysuckle (*Lonicera sempervirens*), which has similar trumpet-shaped flowers but is typically red or yellow.

Cautions: While the flowers and leaves of Orange Honeysuckle are considered safe, the berries should not be consumed, as they may cause mild gastrointestinal upset.

Culinary Preparation: The flower nectar can be sucked directly or used to sweeten teas and other beverages.

Medicinal Properties: Traditionally, Native Americans used the leaves to treat sore throats and respiratory issues. However, there is limited modern research on the medicinal properties of this plant.

Fun Fact: Orange Honeysuckle is a popular garden ornamental plant due to its beautiful, fragrant flowers and ability to attract hummingbirds and butterflies.

Dog Toxicity: No evidence suggests that Orange Honeysuckle is toxic to dogs.

Red Clover
Trifolium pratense [TRY-*FOH*-LEE-UM PRUH-*TEN*-SEE]

Red Clover is a member of the Fabaceae (legume) family. It is also known by other common names such as Meadow Clover, Purple Clover, or Cowgrass.

Location: Originally native to Europe, Western Asia, and northwest Africa, Red Clover has been naturalized in many parts of the world, including North America. It is commonly found in meadows, pastures, and roadsides, thriving in well-drained soils.

Identification:

GROWTH/SIZE: A short-lived perennial herbaceous plant that grows 12-24 inches tall.

BARK/STEM/ROOT: The plant has a hairy, branched stem that emerges from a deep taproot.

LEAF: Red Clover leaves are trifoliate, with three oval leaflets, each having a distinctive V-shaped or crescent-shaped white marking.

FLOWER: The flowers are dense, rounded, pinkish-purple to dark red, and grow at the end of the stems.

FRUIT/SEED/NUT: The fruit is a small, dry pod containing 1-6 seeds.

Look-a-like(s): A non-toxic look-a-like is the White Clover (*Trifolium repens*), which has similar trifoliate leaves but with white or pale pink flowers.

Cautions: Red Clover is generally considered safe for consumption but contains phytoestrogens, which may interact with hormonal medications or cause issues for those with hormone-sensitive conditions.

Culinary Preparation: The flowers and leaves can be used in salads, teas, and soups or as a garnish. The flowers can also be dried and ground into nutritious flour.

Medicinal Properties: Traditionally, Red Clover has been used for its expectorant, anti-inflammatory, and diuretic properties. It is often used as a natural remedy for menopausal symptoms due to its phytoestrogen content.

Fun Fact: Red Clover has been cultivated as a fodder crop for livestock for centuries, as it is a nitrogen-fixing plant that improves soil fertility.

Dog Toxicity: Red Clover is not considered toxic to dogs. However, excessive consumption may cause gastrointestinal upset.

Self-heal
Prunella vulgaris [PROO-NEL-UH VUL-GAIR-ISS]

Self-Heal is a member of the Lamiaceae (mint) family. It is also known by other common names such as Heal-All, Woundwort, or Carpenter's Herb.

Location: Self-Heal is native to Europe, Asia, and North America. It can be found in various habitats, including meadows, lawns, woodland edges, and along roadsides, typically in moist to moderately dry soils.

Identification:

GROWTH/SIZE: A perennial herbaceous plant that grows up to 12 inches tall.

BARK/STEM/ROOT: The plant has square, slender stems that are often creeping at the base and rooting at the nodes.

LEAF: The leaves are opposite, ovate to lanceolate in shape, with serrated edges.

FLOWER: The flowers are tubular, two-lipped, and purple to violet. They are arranged in dense, cylindrical spikes at the top of the stems.

Fʀᴜɪᴛ/Sᴇᴇᴅ/Nᴜᴛ: The fruit is a small, brown, four-sectioned nutlet.

Look-a-like(s): A non-toxic look-a-like is Henbit (*Lamium amplexicaule*), which has a similar flower structure and also belongs to the Lamiaceae family, but its leaves are more rounded and have a scalloped edge.

Cautions: Self-Heal is generally considered safe for consumption, but allergic reactions or individual sensitivities may occur as with any wild plant.

Culinary Preparation: The leaves and flowers can be used in salads, soups, or garnish and can also be made into a refreshing herbal tea.

Medicinal Properties: Traditionally, Self-Heal has been used for its anti-inflammatory, antiseptic, and astringent properties. It was commonly applied topically to treat minor wounds and bruises. Modern research suggests potential benefits for immune system support and antioxidant properties.

Fun Fact: The name "Self-Heal" is derived from the plant's historical use as a versatile healing herb, believed to have the ability to treat a wide variety of ailments.

Dog Toxicity: Self-Heal is not considered toxic to dogs.

Yarrow

Achillea millefolium [UH-KIL-EE-UH MILL-UH-FOH-LEE-UHM]

Yarrow belongs to the Asteraceae (aster or daisy) family and has been used for centuries for its medicinal properties. It is also known as Common Yarrow, Soldier's Woundwort, and Milfoil.

Location: It's native to the Northern Hemisphere, with a wide distribution across North America, Europe, and Asia. It thrives in meadows, fields, and roadsides, preferring sunny areas with well-drained soil.

Identification:

GROWTH/SIZE: A perennial herb, typically growing between 12-36 inches tall.

BARK/STEM/ROOT: The stems are erect, slender, and green, occasionally with a reddish tint. Yarrow roots are fibrous and spread horizontally in the soil.

LEAF: The leaves are feathery and finely divided, resembling a thousand leaflets, hence the species name "millefolium."

Flower: It has flat-topped clusters of small white to pinkish flowers. The inflorescence is a dense, umbrella-like cluster known as a corymb.

Fruit/Seed/Nut: The fruit is a small, dry, one-seeded achene that disperses easily in the wind.

Look-a-like(s): It can be mistaken for Poison Hemlock (*Conium maculatum*), which is a toxic plant. However, Yarrow has a distinct aroma, feathery leaves, and flat-topped flower clusters, while Poison Hemlock has smooth leaves and rounded flower clusters.

Cautions: Yarrow should be used cautiously, as some individuals may be allergic to it, causing skin irritation or other allergic reactions. Pregnant women should avoid using Yarrow, as it may stimulate uterine contractions.

Culinary Preparation: Yarrow leaves can be used fresh or dried as an herb, adding a slightly bitter, aromatic flavor to salads, soups, and teas.

Medicinal Properties: Traditionally, it's been used to treat various ailments, including wounds, fevers, and digestive issues. Modern herbal medicine uses Yarrow for its anti-inflammatory, antispasmodic, and astringent properties. It is often used in teas or tinctures to alleviate cold and flu symptoms, menstrual discomfort, or gastrointestinal problems.

Fun Fact: The name "Achillea" refers to the Greek hero Achilles, who, according to legend, used Yarrow to treat wounds sustained in battle.

Dog Toxicity: Yarrow is not considered toxic to dogs. However, some dogs may have an allergic reaction to the plant.

Yerba Buena
Satureja douglasii [SUH-TURE-EE-JUH DUG-LUH-SEE-EYE]

Yerba Buena is a member of the Lamiaceae (mint) family and is a perennial, aromatic herb known for its medicinal properties. It is also called Western Wild Mint, Oregon Teaberry, and Indian Mint.

Location: Native to the western regions of North America, it can be found from California to British Columbia, thriving in shaded woodlands, grassy slopes, and coastal scrublands.

Identification:

GROWTH/SIZE: A low-growing, creeping plant, reaching heights of 6-12 inches with trailing stems extending up to 3 feet.

BARK/STEM/ROOT: The plant has slender, square stems that are green to reddish-brown, with fibrous roots that spread horizontally.

LEAF: Its leaves are opposite, ovate to heart-shaped, and dark green with a strong minty fragrance when crushed.

FLOWER: Small, tubular, white to pale lavender flowers appear in whorls at the stem tips during spring and summer.

FRUIT/SEED/NUT: The fruit consists of four small nutlets enclosed in the persistent calyx.

Look-a-like(s): It might be confused with other members of the mint family due to its square stem and opposite leaves. However, its distinct aroma and creeping growth habit can help differentiate it from other species.

Cautions: No significant cautions are associated with Yerba Buena.

Culinary Preparation: The leaves can be used fresh or dried to make a refreshing herbal tea with a pleasant minty flavor. The leaves can also be added to salads, soups, or sauces for a burst of flavor.

Medicinal Properties: Traditionally, it has been used by Native Americans and early settlers to treat various ailments, including indigestion, headaches, colds, and rheumatism. The plant is still used in herbal medicine for its antispasmodic, analgesic, and anti-inflammatory properties.

Fun Fact: "Yerba Buena" is Spanish for "good herb," reflecting its widespread use as a medicinal plant by the native people and early settlers of the western United States.

Dog Toxicity: Yerba Buena is not considered toxic to dogs.

White Meadowfoam
Limnanthes alba [LIM-NAAN-THEEZ AL-BUH]

White Meadowfoam is a charming annual wildflower belonging to the Limnanthaceae (meadowfoam) family. Also known as White Marshflower or Poached Egg Plant, this delicate flower is native to the western United States.

Location: White Meadowfoam thrives in vernal pools, wet meadows, and seasonally wet areas in the western United States, particularly California, and Oregon.

Identification:

GROWTH/SIZE: This low-growing plant typically reaches heights of 6-12 inches.

BARK/STEM/ROOT: The plant has slender, branching stems and a shallow, fibrous root system.

LEAF: It features pinnately divided leaves with oblong, toothed leaflets.

FLOWER: The flowers bloom from late winter to early summer, showcasing five white petals with yellow centers, giving them the appearance of poached eggs.

FRUIT/SEED/NUT: After flowering, the plant produces small, capsule-like fruits that contain several seeds.

Look-a-like(s): It might be mistaken for other members of the Limnanthes genus, which share similar flower characteristics. However, its distinctive white petals with yellow centers can help differentiate it from other species.

Cautions: There are no known significant cautions associated with White Meadowfoam.

Culinary Preparation: White Meadowfoam is not widely used in culinary preparations. However, Meadowfoam oil, derived from the seeds, is used as a cooking oil and in salad dressings due to its high antioxidant content and stability.

Medicinal Properties: While there are no widely known medicinal uses for White Meadowfoam, Meadowfoam oil is valued for its cosmetic applications. The oil is used in skin and hair care products due to its moisturizing and conditioning properties.

Fun Fact: Meadowfoam oil, obtained from White Meadowfoam seeds, is also used as an environmentally friendly substitute for petroleum-based oils in various industrial applications.

Dog Toxicity: White Meadowfoam is not considered toxic to dogs.

Western Pearly Everlasting

Anaphalis margaritacea [UH-NAF-UH-LIS MAR-GUH-RIH-TAY-SEE-UH]

Western Pearly Everlasting is a resilient, native wildflower from the Asteraceae (aster or daisy) family. This perennial plant is also known as Pearly Everlasting or Cudweed.

Location: It's found in various habitats, such as meadows, open woodlands, and grasslands. It is native to North America, particularly in the western United States and Canada.

Identification:

GROWTH/SIZE: This robust plant can grow up to 3 feet tall.

BARK/STEM/ROOT:

LEAF: The leaves are narrow, lance-shaped, and grayish-green, with a woolly texture on the underside.

Flower: The flower heads are composed of tiny, pearly-white flowers that bloom from mid-summer to early fall. These flowers have a distinctive, everlasting appearance, retaining their color and shape even after drying.

Fruit/Seed/Nut: The plant produces small, dry, one-seeded fruits called achenes, which are dispersed by the wind.

Look-a-like(s): It may be confused with other species of the Anaphalis genus or similar-looking members of the Asteraceae family. However, the leaf's unique pearly-white flowers and woolly texture help distinguish it from other species.

Cautions: There are no significant cautions associated with Western Pearly Everlasting.

Culinary Preparation: Western Pearly Everlasting is not commonly used in culinary preparations. It is primarily valued for its ornamental and medicinal properties.

Medicinal Properties: Traditionally, Native American tribes used Western Pearly Everlasting for various medicinal purposes, including treating respiratory ailments, digestive issues, and skin conditions. The leaves were often used as a poultice for wounds and burns.

Fun Fact: Western Pearly Everlasting is often used in dried floral arrangements due to its long-lasting, attractive appearance. The flowers retain their color and shape even when dried, making them popular for crafting and home decor.

Dog Toxicity: Western Pearly Everlasting is not considered toxic to dogs.

Western Salsify
Tragopogon dubius [TRUH-GO-PO-GON DOO-BEE-US]

Western Salsify is a biennial plant that belongs to the Asteraceae (aster or daisy) family. This unique wildflower is known by other common names such as Yellow Goatsbeard, Wild Oysterplant, and Meadow Salsify.

Location: It can be found in various habitats, including fields, meadows, and roadsides. Native to Europe and western Asia, it has naturalized across North America and is now widespread across the continent.

Identification:

GROWTH/SIZE: It typically grows between 1 and 4 feet tall.

BARK/STEM/ROOT: The plant has a slender, smooth, hollow stem. Its taproot is long and fleshy, resembling a parsnip or carrot.

LEAF: The leaves are long, narrow, and grass-like, with a blue-green hue. They grow in an alternating pattern along the stem, reaching up to 12 inches long.

FLOWER: It produces large, dandelion-like yellow flowers that close in the afternoon and on cloudy days. The flowers are held atop a long, slender stalk and typically bloom from late spring to early summer.

FRUIT/SEED/NUT: After flowering, the plant produces a round, dandelion-like seed head filled with numerous small, feathery seeds dispersed by the wind.

Look-a-like(s): Yellow Salsify (*Tragopogon pratensis*) is a closely related species that looks very similar to Western Salsify but has a slightly smaller flower head and shorter leaves.

Cautions: There are no significant cautions associated with Western Salsify.

Culinary Preparation: An edible plant with a taste reminiscent of oysters. The roots can be eaten raw or cooked, while the young leaves and flower buds can be added to salads or sautéed as a vegetable.

Medicinal Properties: Historically, Western Salsify has been used to treat digestive issues and as a mild diuretic. However, more research is needed to confirm its effectiveness for these uses.

Fun Fact: Western Salsify was introduced to North America by early European settlers, who cultivated it as a vegetable due to its nutritional value and versatility in the kitchen.

Dog Toxicity: There is no evidence to suggest that Western Salsify is toxic to dogs.

Western Skunk Cabbage
Lysichiton americanus [LIH-SIKH-IH-TON UH-MER-IH-KUH-NUHS]

Western Skunk Cabbage is a unique and unmistakable plant known for its distinctive smell. Belonging to the Araceae (arum or aroid) family, this perennial plant has several other common names, including Swamp Lantern and Yellow Skunk Cabbage.

Location: It can be found in marshy wetlands, swamps, and damp forests. Its native range spans the western parts of North America, from Alaska to California and east to Montana and Idaho.

Identification:

GROWTH/SIZE: A large, robust plant can reach up to 5 feet tall.

BARK/STEM/ROOT: The plant features a thick, fleshy rhizome that anchors it in wet, muddy soil.

LEAF: Large, bright green leaves can grow up to 5 feet long and 3 feet wide. They have a skunky odor when crushed, hence the plant's name.

FLOWER: The unique yellow flower is a modified leaf called a spathe, which surrounds a central spadix. The spadix consists of numerous tiny flowers, and the spathe can reach up to 16 inches tall. The flowers emit a foul odor that attracts pollinating insects.

FRUIT/SEED/NUT: The flowers mature into a cluster of small, berry-like fruits eaten by wildlife, such as birds and bears.

Look-a-like(s): Eastern Skunk Cabbage (*Symplocarpus foetidus*) is a related species in eastern North America. It has a similar appearance, but its spathe is typically maroon or brownish-purple instead of yellow.

Cautions: Western Skunk Cabbage contains calcium oxalate crystals, which can irritate when ingested or handled.

Culinary Preparation: Western Skunk Cabbage is not used for culinary purposes due to its high oxalate content and foul smell.

Medicinal Properties: Traditionally, Native American tribes have used parts of Western Skunk Cabbage for medicinal purposes, including treating respiratory ailments, rheumatism, and skin conditions. However, caution is advised when using this plant for any medicinal purpose due to its potential toxicity.

Fun Fact: Western Skunk Cabbage generates heat through thermogenesis, which helps it melt the surrounding snow and ice, allowing the plant to emerge and bloom early in the spring.

Dog Toxicity: Western Skunk Cabbage is toxic to dogs and can cause symptoms such as drooling, vomiting, diarrhea, and mouth irritation if ingested.

PART SIX
FROM BARK TO NUT
A FLAVORFUL FORAY INTO THE WILD TREES

Scan for full color photos

Beaked Hazelnut
Corylus cornuta [KUH-RIH-LUHS KAWR-NOO-TUH]

Beaked Hazelnut is a deciduous shrub from the Betulaceae (birch) family. This versatile plant is also commonly known as Beaked Filbert and American Hazelnut.

Location: It's native to North America and can be found in various habitats such as forests, woodlands, and thickets. It thrives in moist, well-drained soils and is commonly found in the eastern United States and Canada.

Identification:

GROWTH/SIZE: A multi-stemmed shrub that grows 6 to 16 feet tall.

BARK/STEM/ROOT: The bark is light brown and smooth, with distinctive vertical ridges. The stems are slender and covered with fine hairs.

LEAF: The leaves are oval to heart-shaped, with a serrated margin and pointed tip. They are green on the upper surface and paler beneath, growing 2 to 5 inches.

Flower: It's monoecious, meaning it has both male and female flowers on the same plant. The male flowers are yellowish-brown catkins, while the female flowers are small and red, barely visible among the buds.

Fruit/Seed/Nut: The fruit is a hazelnut encased in a husk with a distinctively elongated, beak-like tip. The nuts ripen in late summer to early fall.

Look-a-like(s): The American Hazelnut (*Corylus americana*) is a similar plant with a rounded, shorter husk surrounding the nut.

Cautions: No significant cautions are associated with Beaked Hazelnuts.

Culinary Preparation: The nuts are edible and can be eaten raw or roasted. They have a sweet, buttery flavor and can be used in various dishes, such as desserts and salads, or enjoyed as a snack.

Medicinal Properties: Indigenous people traditionally use Beaked Hazelnut as an astringent and to treat digestive disorders, although there is limited scientific research to support these uses.

Fun Fact: Native Americans used the Beaked Hazelnut for various purposes, including food, medicine, and making baskets from its flexible branches.

Dog Toxicity: Beaked Hazelnut is not known to be toxic to dogs.

Black Cottonwood
Populus trichocarpa [POH-PYOO-LUHS TRY-KOH-KAR-PUH]

Black Cottonwood is a deciduous tree belonging to the Salicaceae (willow) family. Known for its impressive size and fast growth, it also goes by the names Western Balsam Poplar and California Poplar.

Location: It's native to western North America, particularly in regions with abundant moisture. It can be found along rivers, streams, and lakeshores, as well as in floodplains, riparian forests, and moist woodlands.

Identification:

GROWTH/SIZE: A large, fast-growing tree reaching up to 165 feet tall and 5 feet in diameter.

BARK/STEM/ROOT: The bark is dark gray or brown, becoming deeply furrowed and ridged with age. Young branches are smooth and have a reddish-brown color.

LEAF: The leaves are simple, alternate, and heart-shaped with a pointed tip. They have a dark green upper surface and a lighter green, sometimes silvery, underside. The leaf margins are finely serrated, and the leaves are about 2 to 6 inches long.

FLOWER: It's dioecious, with separate male and female trees. The flowers are arranged in catkins, with the male catkins being reddish and the female catkins greenish.

FRUIT/SEED/NUT: The fruit is a capsule containing numerous small seeds with cotton-like hairs dispersed by the wind.

Look-a-like(s): Other Populus species, such as Eastern Cottonwood (*Populus deltoides*) and Quaking Aspen (*Populus tremuloides*), can be easily confused with Black Cottonwood. Careful examination of the leaves and bark can help differentiate between them.

Cautions: No significant cautions are associated with Black Cottonwood.

Culinary Preparation: Black Cottonwood is not commonly used for culinary purposes.

Medicinal Properties: The resinous buds of Black Cottonwood contain salicin, similar to the active ingredient in aspirin. Traditionally, these buds have been used to treat pain, inflammation, and fever.

Fun Fact: Native Americans used the lightweight, straight-grained wood to construct canoes, paddles, and other tools.

Dog Toxicity: Black Cottonwood is not considered toxic to dogs.

Black Locust
Robinia pseudoacacia [ROH-BIN-EE-UH SOO-DOH-UH-KAY-SHUH]

Black Locust is a deciduous tree from the Fabaceae (legume) family. Native to the southeastern United States, it's known for its hardiness and rapid growth. Black Locust also goes by False Acacia, Yellow Locust, and Green Locust.

Location: Originally native to the southeastern United States, Black Locust has been widely cultivated and naturalized throughout North America and Europe. It can be found in a variety of habitats, from open woodlands to urban areas, and is often used for erosion control and reforestation efforts.

Identification:

GROWTH/SIZE: A medium-sized tree reaching 40 to 100 feet.

BARK/STEM/ROOT: The bark is dark gray to black and deeply furrowed, giving it a characteristic rough texture. The tree has stout, paired spines at the base of the leaves.

Leaf: The leaves are pinnately compound, with 7 to 19 elliptical leaflets 2 to 5 cm (0.8 to 2 inches) long. The leaflets have a smooth edge, dark green on top, and paler green underneath.

Flower: It produces fragrant, white, pea-like flowers that hang in 4 to 8 inches long clusters. They bloom in late spring to early summer.

Fruit/Seed/Nut: The fruit is a flat, brown, bean-like pod, 2 to 4 inches long, containing 4 to 8 seeds. The pods mature in late summer to early fall and can persist on the tree through winter.

Look-a-like(s): Honey Locust (*Gleditsia triacanthos*) is often confused with Black Locust but can be distinguished by its more prominent, branched thorns and bipinnately compound leaves.

Cautions: The bark, leaves, seeds, and young shoots of Black Locusts are toxic due to the presence of toxic compounds called robinin and robitin. Ingestion can cause nausea, vomiting, diarrhea, and even death in severe cases.

Culinary Preparation: Black Locust flowers are edible and can be used to make fritters, syrups, or jellies. Always ensure proper identification and avoid consuming other parts of the tree, as they are toxic.

Medicinal Properties: Historically, the inner bark of Black Locust has been used as an astringent and to treat skin irritations. However, modern usage is limited due to the tree's toxicity.

Fun Fact: Black Locust wood is highly valued for its durability, rot resistance, and strength, making it an ideal choice for fence posts, outdoor furniture, and decking.

Dog Toxicity: Black Locust is toxic to dogs, and ingestion can cause symptoms such as vomiting, diarrhea, weakness, and abdominal pain.

Cascade Mountain Ash

Sorbus scopulina [SORE-BUS SKOH-PYOO-LEE-NUH]

Cascade Mountain Ash is a deciduous tree or shrub belonging to the Rosaceae (rose) family. These native North American species are known as Western Mountain Ash or Greene's Mountain Ash.

Location: It can be found in mountainous regions of western North America, from Alaska to California and eastward to the Rocky Mountains. It typically grows in moist habitats such as streambanks, rocky slopes, and forest edges at 3,300 to 11,500 feet.

Identification:

GROWTH/SIZE: A small tree or large shrub usually grows 6 to 26 feet tall.

BARK/STEM/ROOT: The bark is thin, smooth, and grayish-brown, with vertical fissures on older trunks.

LEAF: The leaves are pinnately compound, with 7 to 15 elliptical, serrated leaflets 1 to 3 inches long. The leaflets are dark green above and paler green beneath.

FLOWER: It blooms in late spring to early summer, producing clusters of small, fragrant, white flowers.

FRUIT/SEED/NUT: The fruit is a small, bright red to orange berry-like pome, 4 to 6 mm in diameter. The fruits mature in late summer to early fall and can persist on the tree into winter.

Look-a-like(s): European Mountain Ash (*Sorbus aucuparia*) is similar in appearance but has more leaflets and larger fruits.

Cautions: The seeds contain small amounts of hydrogen cyanide, which can be toxic if consumed in large quantities. However, the fruits are considered edible when cooked, as the heat destroys the poisonous compounds.

Culinary Preparation: The fruits can make jellies, jams, and sauces. They have a tart flavor and are rich in vitamin C.

Medicinal Properties: Historically, Native Americans used the bark to treat various ailments, including fever, indigestion, and sore throat. The bark is astringent and was also used as a poultice for wounds.

Fun Fact: It's an important food source for wildlife, especially birds. Its colorful fruits provide sustenance for various bird species during the winter months.

Dog Toxicity: No specific reports of dog toxicity related to Cascade Mountain Ash exist. However, the seeds contain hydrogen cyanide, which can be toxic to dogs. Symptoms of cyanide poisoning include difficulty breathing, tremors, seizures, and even death in severe cases.

Lodgepole Pine
Pinus contorta [PIE-NUHS KAWN-TOR-TUH]

The Lodgepole Pine is an evergreen conifer species belonging to the Pinaceae (pine) family. It has several common names, including Shore Pine, Twisted Pine, and Tamarack Pine.

Location: It's native to western North America, from Alaska down to Baja, California, and as far east as the Rocky Mountains. It thrives in various environments, from coastal forests to subalpine areas and from moist, low-lying valleys to dry, rocky slopes.

Identification:

GROWTH/SIZE: Typically grows between 65 to 165 feet tall, with a 1 to 4 feet diameter.

BARK/STEM/ROOT: The bark of young trees is thin and smooth, with a grayish to reddish-brown color. As the tree ages, the bark becomes thicker and develops shallow furrows and irregular, scaly plates.

Leaf: It has needle-like leaves that grow in pairs, each needle being 1 to 3 inches long. The needles are slender, flexible, and dark green.

Flower: This tree produces both male and female cones on the same tree. Male cones are small and yellow, while female cones are green, gradually turning brown as they mature.

Fruit/Seed/Nut: The fruit is a woody cone, which is 1 to 3 inches long and turns brown when mature. Lodgepole Pine cones often remain closed for several years until a fire, high temperatures, or other disturbance triggers their opening to release the seeds.

Look-a-like(s): The Ponderosa Pine (*Pinus ponderosa*) resembles the Lodgepole Pine but has longer needles that grow in bundles of three.

Cautions: There are no specific cautions associated with Lodgepole Pine.

Culinary Preparation: Lodgepole Pine needles can make a vitamin C-rich tea. The inner bark is also edible and can be consumed raw or cooked.

Medicinal Properties: Historically, Native Americans used various parts of the Lodgepole Pine for medicinal purposes. The resin was applied to wounds and skin irritations, and a tea made from the needles was consumed to treat colds and respiratory issues.

Fun Fact: The name "Lodgepole Pine" comes from the tree's traditional use by Native Americans in constructing the poles for their lodges or tipis.

Dog Toxicity: Lodgepole Pine is not considered toxic to dogs.

Oregon Oak
Quercus garryana [KWER-kus GUH-REE-uh-NUH]

The Oregon Oak, also known as Garry Oak or White Oak, is a deciduous tree belonging to the Fagaceae (beech) family. Its history is deeply rooted in the ecology and culture of the Pacific Northwest.

Location: Native to western North America, it primarily grows in the coastal regions of the Pacific Northwest, from southern California up to southwestern British Columbia. It thrives in various habitats, from grassy savannas to mixed woodlands and riverbanks.

Identification:

GROWTH/SIZE: It typically reaches 50 to 100 feet and has a broad, spreading crown.

BARK/STEM/ROOT: The bark is gray to dark gray, becoming deeply furrowed and ridged with age, forming a distinctive checkerboard pattern.

Leaf: The leaves are dark green and lobed, measuring 3 to 6 inches long and 2 to 4 inches wide. The leaves turn a beautiful golden-brown color in the fall before dropping.

Flower: It produces small, inconspicuous flowers called catkins in the spring.

Fruit/Seed/Nut: The fruit is an acorn, approximately 1 to 2 inches long, with a shallow, scaly cap. Acorns mature in a single season and are an essential food source for many wildlife species.

Look-a-like(s): The California Black Oak (*Quercus kelloggii*) can resemble Oregon Oak, but it has leaves with more pointed lobes and a more rounded acorn cap.

Cautions: There are no specific cautions associated with Oregon Oak.

Culinary Preparation: Acorns can be processed to make flour, which can be used in baking or as a thickening agent. The bitter tannins must be leached out before consumption to make the acorns palatable.

Medicinal Properties: Historically, Native Americans used various parts of Oregon Oak for medicinal purposes, including the bark, which was made into a tea to treat diarrhea and stomach ailments.

Fun Fact: Oregon Oak ecosystems support a rich biodiversity, providing habitat for many plant, animal, and insect species, some of which are found nowhere else in the world.

Dog Toxicity: Oregon Oak is not considered toxic to dogs. However, large quantities of acorns ingested by dogs can cause gastrointestinal upset due to the tannins they contain. Symptoms may include vomiting, diarrhea, and abdominal pain. It is best to keep pets from ingesting large acorns to avoid potential issues.

Pacific Crabapple

Malus fusca [MAY-lus FUS-kuh]

Pacific crabapple is native to the Pacific Northwest and is well-adapted to the region's climate and soil. It may not thrive in other regions or areas with extreme temperatures or soil conditions. It's a Rosaceae (rose) family member and is also called the Oregon crabapple.

Locate: It grows in coniferous forests, moist woods, and at the edges of wetlands and estuaries. Moist woods, stream banks, swamps, and bogs in deep rich soils, usually occurring in dense pure thickets.

Identification:

GROWTH/SIZE - typically grows to a height of 20-40 feet, with a spread of 15-30 feet. It has a slow to moderate growth rate and can take up to 20 years to reach its full size.

BARK/STEM/ROOT - The bark is grayish-brown and smooth when young, becoming rough and scaly with age. The stems are slender, with small thorns on younger growth. The root system is shallow, with spreading lateral roots.

Leaf - The leaves are alternate, simple, and ovate-shaped, measuring 2-4 inches long and 1-3 inches wide. They have a serrated edge and are dark green, turning yellow or red in the fall.

Flower - The flowers are pink or white and bloom in early spring before the leaves emerge. They are 1-2 inches wide and arranged in clusters. The flowers have a sweet, fruity fragrance and are pollinated by bees and other insects.

Fruit/Seed/Nut - The fruit is a small, round, red, or yellow apple measuring about 1 inch in diameter. The fruit is edible but sour and is often used for making jams, jellies, and cider. The seeds are tiny and brown, measuring about 0.25 inches long and 0.1 inches wide.

Look-a-like(s): Common Pear (Pyrus communis) has a similar shape, bark, and leaves; however, its flowers are white, and its fruit is larger and more oblong. Common Hawthorn (Crataegus monogyna) has similar leaves, flowers, and fruit; however, its fruit is smaller and more berry-like, and its branches have thorns.

Caution: The fruit is edible but sour and may cause digestive upset if consumed in large quantities. Additionally, the fruit seeds contain trace amounts of cyanide, although the amount is not considered harmful to humans.

Culinary Preparation: The pome fruits ripen in August and September but can remain on the tree well into the winter. It's often used for making jams, jellies, and cider. The fruit can make tangy and flavorful vinegar, pies, tarts, and other baked goods.

Medicinal Properties: Indigenous peoples of the Pacific Northwest valued crabapple fruits as a food source and gathered them all along the coast. Analgesics and stomach problems have been treated with infusions of this traditional medicinal plant's bark and fruit.

Fun Fact: It has a vital cultural significance for many indigenous tribes in the Pacific Northwest, who use the tree in ceremonies and as a symbol of resilience and strength.

Dog Toxicity: Generally, fruit is safe to consume in small amounts. The fruit is edible but sour and may cause digestive upset if consumed in large quantities. Interestingly, the seeds also contain cyanide, but the amount is not considered dangerous for dogs.

Pacific Madrone

Arbutus menziesii [AHR-BYOO-TUHS MEN-ZEE-ZEE-EYE]

Pacific Madrone is an evergreen tree from the Ericaceae (heath or heather) family. It is also commonly known as Madrona, Madrone, or Arbutus. The tree is admired for its unique appearance, making it an iconic species of the Pacific Northwest.

Location: Native to the coastal areas of western North America, Pacific Madrone can be found from southern Alaska down to Baja California. It typically grows on dry, rocky slopes and well-drained soils in coastal forests and woodlands.

Identification:

GROWTH/SIZE: It can reach heights of 40 to 100 feet, with an irregular, spreading crown.

BARK/STEM/ROOT: The most striking feature is its reddish-orange, peeling bark, which reveals a smooth, greenish-gray layer underneath. The bark exfoliates throughout the year.

LEAF: The leaves are thick, leathery, and oval-shaped, measuring 3 to 6 inches long. The upper surface is dark green and glossy, while the underside is a lighter, matte green.

FLOWER: In spring, it produces clusters of small, bell-shaped, white to pinkish flowers.

FRUIT/SEED/NUT: The fruit is a small, round, orange-to-red berry measuring 1/4 to 1/2 inch in diameter. The berries are edible and are consumed by various wildlife species.

Look-a-like(s): Pacific Madrone may be confused with other Arbutus species, such as the Texas Madrone (*Arbutus xalapensis*), which has similar bark and leaves. However, the Texas Madrone is native to the southwestern United States and Mexico and is not found in the Pacific Northwest.

Cautions: There are no specific cautions associated with Pacific Madrone.

Culinary Preparation: The berries can be eaten raw or cooked, although they have a slightly astringent taste. They can be used to make jams, jellies, and beverages.

Medicinal Properties: Indigenous peoples have traditionally used Pacific Madrone for various medicinal purposes. The leaves were made into a tea to treat stomach ailments and sore throats, while the bark was used to alleviate skin irritations and infections.

Fun Fact: Pacific Madrone trees are known for their ability to grow in a twisted, contorted manner, making them an intriguing subject for photographers and artists.

Dog Toxicity: Pacific Madrone is not considered toxic to dogs.

Paperbark Birch

Betula papyrifera [BEH-TOO-LUH PAH-PUH-RIFF-ER-UH]

Paperbark Birch is a deciduous tree belonging to the Betulaceae (birch) family. It has a few other common names, like Canoe Birch or White Birch, that hint at its appearance and historical uses.

Location: Native to North America, it thrives in cooler climates and can be found from Alaska to Newfoundland, extending southward to the northeastern United States. These trees prefer moist, well-drained soils in sunny locations.

Identification:

GROWTH/SIZE: It usually grows between 65 to 100 feet tall, with a slender trunk and a graceful, open crown.

BARK/STEM/ROOT: The tree's show-stopping feature is its creamy-white, peeling bark that gives it a paper-like appearance. The bark naturally exfoliates in thin, horizontal strips, revealing a pinkish or orange-brown inner layer.

Leaf: The leaves are alternately arranged, oval to triangular, and measure 2 to 4 inches long. The leaf edges are double-toothed, and the leaf surface is a bright green, turning yellow in the fall.

Flower: It produces catkins in the spring, with separate male and female flowers on the same tree. Male catkins are long and pendulous, while female catkins are shorter and more upright.

Fruit/Seed/Nut: The fruit is a small, winged nutlet dispersed by wind. The nutlets are enclosed in cone-like structures that disintegrate upon maturity.

Look-a-like(s): It may be confused with other birch species, like the European White Birch (*Betula pendula*), which also has white bark. However, the European White Birch has more drooping branches and a slightly different leaf shape.

Cautions: There are no specific cautions associated with Paperbark Birch.

Culinary Preparation: Paperbark Birch sap can be tapped and used as a refreshing drink or boiled down to make birch syrup. The tender young leaves and catkins can be eaten raw or cooked, adding a unique flavor to salads or stir-fries.

Medicinal Properties: Traditionally, Native Americans used Paperbark Birch for various medicinal purposes. The sap was believed to have detoxifying properties and treat skin conditions, while the inner bark was used to make a poultice for wounds and inflammations.

Fun Fact: The Paperbark Birch's lightweight and waterproof bark made it an ideal material for Native Americans to construct canoes, earning it the nickname "Canoe Birch."

Dog Toxicity: Paperbark Birch is not considered toxic to dogs.

Sitka Spruce
Picea sitchensis [PIH-SEE-UH SIT-CHEN-SIS]

Sitka Spruce is a mighty conifer from the Pinaceae (pine) family. This evergreen giant is known as Tideland Spruce, Coast Spruce, or Menzies Spruce, showcasing its affinity for coastal environments.

Location: It's native to the Pacific Northwest and predominantly found along the coastal regions of Alaska, British Columbia, Washington, Oregon, and Northern California. This tree thrives in moist, cool climates, often growing near bodies of water and in foggy, misty conditions.

Identification:

GROWTH/SIZE: This is the tallest of all spruce species, reaching staggering heights of up to 330 feet, with trunks measuring over 16 feet in diameter. These magnificent trees can live for over 700 years as silent witnesses to centuries of history.

BARK/STEM/ROOT: The bark is thin, scaly, and grayish-brown. As the tree ages, the bark may develop furrows and ridges, creating a more rugged appearance.

LEAF: The leaves are needle-like, measuring 1/2 to 1 inch long, and exhibit a bluish-green color. The needles are attached to the twig via a small peg-like structure, making them appear somewhat crowded.

FLOWER: It's monoecious, producing male and female cones on the same tree. Male cones are small and reddish-brown, while female cones are more prominent, cylindrical, and green, turning brown when mature.

FRUIT/SEED/NUT: Mature female cones release winged seeds dispersed by the wind, allowing the Sitka Spruce to propagate over considerable distances.

Look-a-like(s): Sitka Spruce can be confused with Engelmann Spruce (*Picea engelmannii*), which shares a similar appearance. However, Engelmann Spruce has a more inland distribution and can be distinguished by its lighter blue-green needles and less densely packed branching.

Cautions: There are no specific cautions associated with Sitka Spruce.

Culinary Preparation: It's not widely used in culinary preparations, but its young, tender tips can be harvested in spring and used to make a refreshing, citrusy tea or added to salads for a unique twist.

Medicinal Properties: Traditional medicinal uses include chewing the resin to treat sore throats and colds and brewing tea from the needles as a source of vitamin C. The resin is also antimicrobial and has been used to treat wounds and skin conditions.

Fun Fact: During World War II, Sitka Spruce was used in aircraft construction thanks to its impressive strength-to-weight ratio. The famous British fighter plane, the Supermarine Spitfire, utilized Sitka Spruce in its airframe design.

Dog Toxicity: Sitka Spruce is not considered toxic to dogs.

Subalpine Fir
Abies lasiocarpa [AY-BEEZ LASS-EE-OH-KAR-PUH]

Subalpine Fir is a majestic evergreen conifer that belongs to the Pinaceae (pine) family. Depending on the location and specific subspecies, this high-altitude specialist is also known as Rocky Mountain Fir, White Fir, or Corkbark Fir.

Location: It's native to the mountainous regions of western North America, ranging from Alaska down to New Mexico. This tree prefers the colder climates of high elevations, often dominating the landscape near or above the treeline.

Identification:

GROWTH/SIZE: A medium-sized tree, reaching heights of 65 to 130 feet with a slender, spire-like crown. Its symmetrical appearance makes it popular for Christmas trees and ornamental plantings.

BARK/STEM/ROOT: The bark is smooth and grayish-white when young, becoming rougher and more furrowed. The branches are covered with short, stiff needles that point upwards.

LEAF: The needles are flat, measuring 1/4 to 1 inch long, and exhibit a blue-green color with a white, waxy coating. The needles are arranged spirally around the branch but twist at their base to form a flattened, upturned appearance.

FLOWER: It's monoecious, producing male and female cones on the same tree. Male cones are small and yellowish, while female cones are larger, cylindrical, and purple, eventually turning brown when mature.

FRUIT/SEED/NUT: Mature female cones release winged seeds dispersed by the wind, allowing the Subalpine Fir to colonize new territories in high-elevation environments.

Look-a-like(s): It can be confused with Engelmann Spruce (*Picea engelmannii*), which shares a similar habitat preference. Their needles can distinguish the two: Subalpine Fir has flat, upturned needles, while Engelmann Spruce has sharp, square needles.

Cautions: There are no specific cautions associated with Subalpine Fir.

Culinary Preparation: Subalpine Fir is not widely used in culinary preparations, but the young, tender tips can be harvested in spring and used to make a fragrant, refreshing tea.

Medicinal Properties: Traditionally, Subalpine Fir needles have been used to make a tea high in vitamin C. The resin has been applied to wounds and skin irritations for its antimicrobial properties.

Fun Fact: Subalpine Fir trees are crucial in providing habitat for various bird species, such as the threatened White-tailed Ptarmigan, which relies on the tree for cover and nesting sites.

Dog Toxicity: Subalpine Fir is not considered toxic to dogs.

Western Chokecherry

Prunus virginiana demissa [PROO-NUS VER-JIN-EE-AY-NUH DUH-MISS-UH]

Western Chokecherry is a delightful deciduous shrub belonging to the Rosaceae (rose) family. Known for its beautiful but astringent fruit, this plant is also called Bitter-berry, Virginia Bird Cherry, or simply Chokecherry.

Location: It's native to the western regions of North America, spanning from British Columbia and Alberta down to California, Arizona, and New Mexico. It thrives in various habitats, from moist stream banks and canyon bottoms to dry slopes and open woodlands.

Identification:

GROWTH/SIZE: A medium-sized shrub, typically reaching heights of 6 to 16 feet. It often forms dense thickets, providing valuable cover and nesting sites for various wildlife species.

BARK/STEM/ROOT: The bark is thin and smooth, with a grayish-brown color that becomes more furrowed as the shrub ages.

Leaf: The leaves are simple, elliptical, and finely toothed, measuring 1 to 4 inches long. They are dark green on the upper surface and lighter green beneath, turning yellow or red in the fall.

Flower: This shrub produces small, fragrant, white flowers in elongated clusters (racemes) in late spring.

Fruit/Seed/Nut: It's known for its small, dark purple to black fruit.

Look-a-like(s): Western Chokecherry can be confused with Black Cherry (*Prunus serotina*) or Common Chokecherry (*Prunus virginiana*). The key to differentiating them is examining the leaves: Western Chokecherry has leaves with rounded bases, while the other two species have more pointed or tapered ones.

Cautions: Western Chokecherry's seeds, leaves, and twigs contain cyanogenic glycosides, which can release cyanide when ingested. Consuming large amounts of these plant parts can be toxic, so caution is advised when harvesting the fruit.

Culinary Preparation: Despite their bitterness, Western Chokecherries can be used in various culinary applications, such as jellies, jams, syrups, and wines. The cherries are quite astringent when raw but become sweeter when cooked.

Medicinal Properties: Native American tribes have traditionally used Western Chokecherry bark to treat various ailments, including coughs, colds, and gastrointestinal issues. The bark contains natural compounds with anti-inflammatory and antioxidant properties, though more research is needed to confirm its medicinal efficacy.

Fun Fact: Western Chokecherries have played a crucial role in the diets of various Native American tribes, who used them not only as a food source but also to dye fabric and basketry materials.

Dog Toxicity: Western Chokecherry can be toxic to dogs if they consume large quantities of leaves, seeds, or twigs. Poisoning symptoms may include difficulty breathing, excessive drooling, vomiting, and diarrhea.

Hey there, reader! Have you ever stumbled upon a book that sparked your interest and provided a valuable experience that you couldn't help but share with others? If so, you know how satisfying it can be to pass that knowledge and joy. And that's exactly why I'm here today - to ask you to consider leaving a review for the book "Wild Edible Plants of the Pacific Northwest."

Now, I know what you're thinking. "Why should I bother leaving a review?" Well, my friends, the answer is simple: by sharing your thoughts and experiences, you can help others find the same joy and fulfillment you did while reading this book.

Think about it - have you ever hesitated to try something new, like foraging for wild edibles, because you didn't know where to start or what to look for? Your review can be the guiding light for someone else who is just beginning on their wild edible adventure. By sharing your insights and opinions, you can give others the confidence to try something new and potentially life-changing.

Not to mention, leaving a review is incredibly easy! Head to Amazon and find the book's listing. You can leave a rating and write a brief review detailing your thoughts and opinions.

But let's talk about the real reason we're here - the impact your review can have on others. Your review could be the deciding factor for someone who is on the fence about whether or not to buy this book. It could be the one thing that convinces them to take the plunge and embark on their wild edible adventure.

And let's remember your review's impact on the author. By leaving a positive review, you're not only helping others but also showing your support and appreciation for the hard work and dedication that went into creating this book.

So, what are you waiting for? Go leave a review for "Wild Edible Plants of the Pacific Northwest" and share your thoughts and experiences with the world. Who knows - you could introduce someone to a new world of adventure and exploration. And who doesn't love a little bit of goodwill and positive karma in their lives?

PART SEVEN
FOREST FUNGI FEAST
AN INTRODUCTION TO WILD MUSHROOMS

The experience of mushroom foraging can be rewarding and fun. However, it is essential to correctly identify mushrooms before consuming them. Learning how to identify mushrooms by using field guides, taking foraging classes, or observing experienced foragers is critical. You should pay close attention to the cap, stem, and gills' shape, color, and texture. It is also crucial to consider the mushroom's habitat and the plants and trees it grows near.

Many poisonous mushrooms can cause severe illness or even death if ingested. Whenever you are foraging, stay away from mushrooms with white gills. Additionally, many poisonous mushrooms have red pigmentation on their cap or stem.

Whenever possible, be cautious and only consume mushrooms that an expert has positively identified. It would be best never to eat raw mushrooms because some toxic mushrooms can cause severe reactions. It is also important to remember that even though the mushroom is edible, some people will still experience allergic reactions. Therefore, starting small is essential when trying a new mushroom species.

It is generally recommended that dogs not be allowed to eat wild mushrooms, as it can be challenging to identify toxic species, and even a tiny amount of a poisonous mushroom can be harmful to a dog. It is best to err on the side of caution and keep your dog away from wild mushrooms.

Scan for full color photos

Bear's Head Tooth

Hericium americanum [HUH-*RIH*-SEE-UM UH-MAIR-UH-*KAN*-UHM]

Bear's Head Tooth is a fascinating mushroom belonging to the Hericiaceae (tooth fungi) family. With its distinctive appearance, this edible fungus is also known as the Lion's Mane, the Bearded Tooth Mushroom, or the Satyr's Beard.

Location: Bear's Head Tooth is native to North America, primarily in the United States and Canada. It grows on the deadwood or wounds of hardwood trees, mainly oak and beech, in eastern deciduous and mixed coniferous forests.

Identification:

CAP - It lacks a traditional mushroom cap. Instead, it has a densely packed mass of downward-hanging, white to cream-colored spines that resemble a shaggy, tooth-like structure or the mane of a lion.

Hymenium - The hymenium, or spore-producing surface, is located on the outer surface of the spines. As the mushroom matures, the spines may turn yellowish-brown or grayish.

Stipe - This mushroom typically does not have a well-defined stipe (stem), as the spines grow directly from the tree or substrate.

Spore print - The spore print is white, a crucial identifier distinguishing it from similar species.

Ecology - Bear's Head Tooth is a saprotrophic fungus that decomposes dead organic material. It is vital in breaking down deadwood and recycling nutrients in forest ecosystems.

Look-a-like(s): The primary look-a-like for Bear's Head Tooth is another edible mushroom called the Comb Tooth (*Hericium coralloides*). The main difference is that the Comb Tooth has more extended, branched spines, while the Bear's Head Tooth has shorter, more compact spines.

Cautions: It's considered a safe and edible mushroom. However, always exercise caution when foraging mushrooms and consult an expert or a reliable field guide to ensure proper identification.

Culinary Preparation: Bear's Head Tooth has a delicate, seafood-like flavor reminiscent of crab or lobster. It can be sautéed in butter, added to soups, or used as a topping for pasta dishes. The mushroom's tender, meaty texture makes it a delicious and versatile ingredient in various recipes.

Medicinal Properties: Bear's Head Tooth has been used in traditional medicine for its potential anti-inflammatory, antioxidant, and cognitive-enhancing properties. Modern research is exploring its potential benefits for improving memory, supporting nerve regeneration, and promoting overall brain health.

Fun Fact: Bear's Head Tooth has been used in traditional Chinese medicine for centuries to treat various ailments, including stomach issues and ulcers. Today, it continues to be a popular functional food and dietary supplement in many parts of the world.

Candy Cap
Lactarius rubidus [LUH-KTEER-EE-UHS ROO-BAHY-DUHS]

The Candy Cap is a unique mushroom belonging to the family of Russulaceae (brittle gill or milk cap). What sets it apart from other mushrooms is its distinct maple syrup-like aroma when dried. It's also known by other names such as the Curry Milkcap or the Maple Sugar Mushroom.

Location: Candy Cap mushrooms are primarily found along the west coast of North America, ranging from northern California to the Pacific Northwest. They grow in coniferous forests, favoring damp, mossy areas, and can be found fruiting from late fall to early winter.

Identification:

CAP - The cap is small to medium-sized, typically 1-3 inches long. It is convex in shape when young, eventually flattening out with age. The cap color ranges from orange-brown to reddish-brown and can be slightly sticky when moist.

Hymenium - The hymenium consists of closely spaced gills attached to the stipe. Gills are cream to pale yellow in color, sometimes turning pinkish with age.

Stipe - The stipe is cylindrical, relatively slender, and about the same length as the cap's diameter. It is typically cream to pale yellow, sometimes with a faint pinkish hue.

Spore print - The spore print is white to pale cream, which can help differentiate it from some of its look-a-likes.

Ecology - Candy Cap mushrooms are mycorrhizal, meaning they form a symbiotic relationship with the roots of certain trees, particularly conifers like pine, Douglas fir, and hemlock.

Look-a-like(s): Candy Cap mushrooms have several non-toxic look-a-likes, including Golden milkcap (*Lactarius xanthogalactus*) and Sticky cap (*Lactarius subviscidus*). However, their distinguishing feature is the strong maple syrup scent when dried, which the look-a-likes do not possess.

Cautions: Candy Cap mushrooms are considered safe to eat, but always exercise caution when foraging for wild mushrooms. Consult a reliable field guide or an expert to ensure proper identification.

Culinary Preparation: Candy Cap mushrooms are famous for their sweet, maple-like aroma and are often used in desserts like cookies, cakes, and ice cream. They can also be added to savory dishes for a unique twist, such as risottos, soups, or sauces.

Medicinal Properties: While they are primarily valued for their culinary uses, they contain antioxidants and other beneficial compounds in many edible mushrooms. However, no specific evidence supports this species' unique medicinal properties.

Fun Fact: Candy Cap mushrooms have been used by indigenous peoples along the west coast of North America as a natural sweetener and flavoring agent. The strong maple scent is due to a compound called quabalactone III, which develops when the mushroom is dried.

Coral Tooth Fungus
Hericium coralloides [HEH-RIH-SEE-UM KOR-UH-LOY-DEEZ]

Meet the Coral Tooth Fungus, an oddball among mushrooms with its unique, coral-like appearance. This fascinating fungus belongs to the Hericiaceae (tooth fungi) family and is sometimes called the Comb Tooth or the Bear's Head Tooth's spiny cousin.

Location: It's found throughout North America, Europe, and Asia, often at higher elevations. It prefers to grow on decaying hardwood logs or stumps, mainly beech and oak, so keep an eye out when hiking through temperate forests.

Identification:

CAP - Forget about traditional caps with this funky fungus. Instead, it sports branched, coral-like structures with numerous spine-like projections hanging downwards.

Hymenium - The hymenium is found on the downward-pointing teeth or spines, up to 1 inch long. These spines are responsible for producing and releasing the fungus's spores.

Stipe - There's no real stipe on this mushroom. It directly attaches to the wood it's growing on, with the branched structures emerging from the attachment point.

Spore print - The spore print is white, a common trait among many toothed fungi.

Ecology - This fungus is a saprophyte, which breaks down dead organic matter, playing an essential role in recycling nutrients in forest ecosystems.

Look-a-like(s): It's often confused with its relatives, such as the Bear's Head Tooth (*Hericium americanum*) and the Lion's Mane (*Hericium erinaceus*). While they share similarities in growth habits and edibility, their distinct shapes set them apart.

Cautions: While the Coral Tooth Fungus is considered edible, proper identification is vital when foraging for mushrooms. Always consult an expert or use a trusted field guide.

Culinary Preparation: It has a mild, slightly sweet flavor and a delicate texture. It's best cooked, such as sautéed in butter or used in soups and stews. It's essential to cook it thoroughly, as it can be slightly bitter when raw.

Medicinal Properties: Some of the reported medicinal uses and potential health benefits of Hericium coralloides include neuroprotective and neuroregenerative properties, which help improve cognitive function, memory, and learning abilities.

Fun Fact: Although the Coral Tooth Fungus is not as well-known as its Lion's Mane and Bear's Head Tooth cousins, it has made its mark in mycology. Its bizarre, coral-like appearance has earned it a reputation as one of the most intriguing fungi in the woods.

Saffron Milk Cap
Lactarius deliciosus [LAK-TARE-EE-US DEE-LIH-KOH-SUS]

Introducing the Saffron Milk Cap, a colorful, charismatic mushroom belonging to the Russulaceae (brittle gill or milk cap) family. Its vivid hues, and delectable taste has earned it various common names, such as the Red Pine Mushroom, the Delicious Milk Cap, and the Orange Latex Milky.

Location: It's widely distributed across North America, Europe, and Asia. This mycorrhizal fungus forms a symbiotic relationship with coniferous trees, mainly pines. So, when exploring pine forests, watch for this golden gem.

Identification:

CAP - The cap is a sight to behold! With its orange to reddish-orange hues and greenish tinges, it has a slightly convex shape that flattens over time—the cap measures 3 to 6 inches in diameter.

Hymenium - Beneath the cap, you'll find closely spaced gills slightly decurrent, extending slightly down the stipe. When damaged, they release a milky, orange-red latex, hence its name.

Stipe - The stipe is cylindrical, stout, and ranges from 1 to 3 inches long. It's usually the same color as the cap, with greenish or blueish tinges.

Spore print - It produces an ochre or pale yellow spore print, adding to its colorful appeal.

Ecology - As a mycorrhizal fungus, it forms a mutually beneficial relationship with coniferous trees, helping them absorb nutrients while receiving sugars in return.

Look-a-like(s): The Saffron Milk Cap has a few look-a-likes, such as Orange Milkcap (*Lactarius deterrimus*) and Bleeding Milkcap (*Lactarius semisanguifluus*). These species are not toxic but are considered less palatable.

Cautions: Always be cautious and consult an expert or a reliable field guide when foraging mushrooms. Remember that the Saffron Milk Cap's key identification features include vivid colors, decurrent gills, and orange-red latex.

Culinary Preparation: A popular edible mushroom with a slightly nutty flavor and a firm, chewy texture. It's best sautéed in butter, added to soups, or used as a pizza topping. Ensure to cook it well, as it can be slightly bitter when raw.

Medicinal Properties: Though not widely known for its medicinal properties, the Saffron Milk Cap is rich in antioxidants and traditionally used to support general health and well-being.

Fun Fact: The Saffron Milk Cap's vibrant colors and delicious taste have made it a sought-after prize among foragers. It's so well-loved in some regions that annual festivals celebrate the mushroom, with people gathering to hunt, cook, and share the tasty morsels with fellow enthusiasts.

Shaggy Parasol

Chlorophyllum rhacodes [KLOR-OH-FIL-UM RA-KO-DEEZ]

Meet the Shaggy Parasol, a fascinating mushroom with a funky appearance that makes it stand out from the crowd. It belongs to the Agaricaceae family and is known by other names such as Shaggy Mane and Shaggy Pholiota.

Location: It can be found across North America, Europe, and other parts of the world. This fascinating fungus prefers nutrient-rich soil and is often spotted in grasslands, parks, and forest edges, sometimes even in well-manicured lawns.

Identification:

CAP - Sporting an eye-catching, shaggy, and scaly surface, the cap is typically light brown to cream. As it matures, the cap expands, reaching a 4 to 12 inches diameter.

HYMENIUM - It features free gills, meaning they don't attach to the stipe. The gills are initially white but become cream-colored as the mushroom matures.

Stipe - The stipe is long, thick, and white with a bulbous base. A distinctive feature of this mushroom is its double ring, which is movable along the stipe.

Spore print - The spore print is white, making it easy to identify among its colorful counterparts.

Ecology - It's a saprobic fungus that feeds on decaying organic matter, playing a crucial role in ecosystem nutrient recycling.

Look-a-like(s): The Shaggy Parasol has a toxic look-a-like, the False Parasol (*Chlorophyllum molybdites*), which causes gastrointestinal distress when consumed. The critical difference between the two is the greenish spore print of the False Parasol, compared to the white spore print of the Shaggy Parasol.

Cautions: Proper identification is essential when foraging for Shaggy Parasols. Always consult an expert or a reliable field guide. Some individuals may experience gastrointestinal upset after consuming this mushroom, so it's important to try a small amount first to gauge your body's reaction.

Culinary Preparation: The Shaggy Parasol is an edible mushroom with a pleasant, nutty flavor. It's best cooked thoroughly, sautéed in butter, or used in soups, stews, and risottos. Due to its large size, it also makes a fantastic substitute for Portobello mushrooms in various dishes.

Medicinal Properties: While the Shaggy Parasol doesn't boast significant medicinal properties, it is a nutritious and delicious addition to a healthy diet.

Fun Fact: The Shaggy Parasol's impressive appearance and unique characteristics have made it a popular subject for artists and photographers, who often capture its beauty in stunning, detailed images that showcase the intricate patterns and textures of this marvelous mushroom.

Turkey Tail

Trametes versicolor [TRUH-MEE-TEEZ VUR-SI-KUH-LUR]

The Turkey Tail is a polypore mushroom with a colorful, fan-shaped appearance. This fungus is part of the Polyporaceae (bracket fungi) family and is often called the Many-Zoned Polypore or the Cloud Mushroom.

Location: It's a cosmopolitan mushroom throughout North America, Europe, Asia, and beyond. It thrives on decaying logs, stumps, and branches in various forest environments, making it a captivating sight during woodland walks.

Identification:

Cap - The cap is small, colorful, and fan-shaped, resembling a turkey's tail feathers. Its concentric zones feature shades of brown, gray, blue, and even purple, with a velvety surface and white edges.

Hymenium - On the underside of the cap, it features small, round pores that release spores. The pore surface is typically white to beige.

Stipe - It does not have a stipe, as they grow directly from the wood in a shelf-like formation.

Spore Print - The spore print is white

Ecology - As a saprophytic fungus, it breaks down dead organic matter, contributing to nutrient recycling in forest ecosystems.

Look-a-like(s): The False Turkey Tail (*Stereum ostrea*) is a non-toxic look-a-like that its smooth, poreless underside can distinguish. Another similar species is the Violet Toothed Polypore (*Trichaptum biforme*), which has a purple-tinged, toothed underside.

Cautions:

Culinary Preparation: Turkey Tail is not considered a culinary mushroom due to its tough, leathery texture. However, it is often used to make teas and extracts valued for their potential health benefits.

Medicinal Properties: Turkey Tail has been used in traditional medicine for centuries and is currently being studied for its potential immune-boosting and anti-cancer properties. The fungus contains polysaccharides believed to enhance the immune system and inhibit tumor growth.

Fun Fact: Turkey Tail has a long history in traditional Chinese medicine, where it's known as Yun Zhi. This mushroom has been used for its health-promoting properties for over 1,000 years, making it an essential part of ancient healing practices.

West Coast Reishi

Ganoderma oregonense [GUH-NOH-DER-MUH OH-RUH-GAHN-ENSE]

West Coast Reishi is an extraordinary mushroom that graces the Pacific coast with its presence. This fascinating fungus belongs to the Ganodermataceae family and is known by several other common names, such as the Oregon Reishi or Western Hemlock Varnish Shelf.

Location: It's native to the Pacific Northwest region of North America, from California to Alaska. It predominantly grows on coniferous trees, particularly on dead or dying Western Hemlock, and can be found in coastal forests and along riverbanks.

Identification:

CAP - The cap is kidney-shaped or semicircular, displaying a glossy, reddish-brown surface that looks like it's been varnished. The cap can grow up to 12 inches in diameter and often features a white or cream-colored margin.

HYMENIUM - The underside of the cap is covered in tiny, creamy white pores that release spores as the mushroom matures.

Stipe - It has a short, stout stipe that is typically off-center and attached to the cap. The stipe shares the cap's glossy, varnished appearance.

Spore print - The spore print is brown.

Ecology - As a wood-decay fungus, West Coast Reishi plays a vital role in breaking down dead organic matter in its forest habitat.

Look-a-like(s): The Red Reishi (*Ganoderma lucidum*) is a non-toxic look-a-like that can be distinguished by its smaller size and preference for growing on hardwood trees. The Artist's Conk (*Ganoderma applanatum*) is another similar species, but it lacks the glossy, varnished appearance of West Coast Reishi.

Cautions: It can cause gastrointestinal discomfort in some individuals and may interact with certain medications, such as blood thinners, immunosuppressants, and some chemotherapy drugs.

Culinary Preparation: West Coast Reishi is not typically consumed as a culinary mushroom due to its tough, woody texture. However, it is commonly used to make teas, tinctures, and extracts that are valued for their potential health benefits.

Medicinal Properties: Like other Ganoderma species, West Coast Reishi has a long history of medicinal use in various cultures. It is believed to have immune-boosting, anti-inflammatory, and antioxidant properties. Modern research investigates its potential to support overall health and combat multiple illnesses.

Fun Fact: The term "Reishi" is derived from the Japanese word "Rei," meaning divine or spiritual, and "Shi," which refers to a mushroom. This revered name reflects the long-standing belief in the mushroom's ability to promote well-being and longevity, earning it a place in the pantheon of medicinal fungi.

Western Yellowfoot

Craterellus tubaeformis [KRAH-TUH-RELL-UHS TOO-BAY-FOR-MISS]

Western Yellowfoot is a charming little mushroom that brightens up the forest floor. This delectable fungi belong to the Cantharellaceae (chanterelle) family and goes by other common names such as Yellowfoot Chanterelle or Winter Chanterelle.

Location: It's found in the Pacific Northwest region of North America and extends into parts of Europe. This mushroom prefers wet, mossy coniferous forests, often appearing near streams or mountainous areas during fall and winter.

Identification:

CAP - The cap is convex to flat, with a wavy, irregular margin. Its color ranges from brownish-yellow to grayish-brown, and the cap can reach up to 2 inches in diameter.

Hymenium - The underside of the cap features false gills, which are blunt ridges that run down the stipe. These ridges are typically the same color as the cap or slightly paler.

Stipe - The stipe is hollow, slender, and can grow up to 4 inches tall. It exhibits a vibrant yellow color, hence the name "Yellowfoot."

Spore print - The spore print of this mushroom is pale yellow to yellowish-white, helping to distinguish it from other species.

Ecology - Western Yellowfoot mushrooms are mycorrhizal, forming beneficial relationships with the roots of nearby trees, especially conifers.

Look-a-like(s): The Western Yellowfoot can be confused with the non-toxic Cantharellus species, such as the Golden Chanterelle (*Cantharellus cibarius*). However, the Golden Chanterelle has a more vibrant orange color and a thicker, less hollow stipe.

Cautions: Accurate identification is crucial when foraging for any wild mushroom. Consult an expert or a reputable field guide before consuming any wild mushroom to avoid potential toxic look-a-likes.

Culinary Preparation: It's a culinary treat, boasting a mild, earthy flavor and a slightly crunchy texture. It is best enjoyed when sautéed in butter or oil, added to soups, stews, or pasta dishes, or used as a delightful topping on toast.

Medicinal Properties: Although not explicitly known for its medicinal properties, the Western Yellowfoot is a good source of nutrients, providing vitamins, minerals, and dietary fiber that contribute to overall health.

Fun Fact: Western Yellowfoot mushrooms are famous for their ability to withstand freezing temperatures, earning them the nickname "Winter Chanterelle." It's not uncommon for foragers to find these resilient mushrooms peeking through the snow, offering a colorful surprise during the colder months.

Wood Ear
Auricularia polytricha [AW-RIK-YUH-LAIR-EE-UH PAH-LEE-TRY-KUH]

Wood Ear is fungi that are as fun to touch as it is to say! This unique mushroom is part of the Auriculariaceae (wood ear) family and also goes by the names Jelly Ear, Judas's Ear, or Tree Ear, which allude to its distinctive appearance.

Location: It's cosmopolitan, found on decaying wood around the globe, particularly on elder trees. This fungus enjoys damp, shaded environments in forests and woodlands across North America, Europe, and Asia.

Identification:

CAP - The cap is gelatinous, ear-shaped, and can range from 1 to 4 inches in size. It boasts a velvety, dark brown to reddish-brown hue on the outer surface, while the inner surface is lighter and smooth.

HYMENIUM - The hymenium is the smooth, lighter-colored inner part of the cap. It is free from gills or pores, contributing to the mushroom's jelly-like appearance.

Stipe - It's often sessile, meaning it lacks a stipe. When present, the stipe is short, rudimentary, and attaches to the wood at the cap's narrow end.

Spore print - A white spore print distinguishes the Wood Ear from other similar species.

Ecology - The Wood Ear is a saprotrophic fungus, feeding on decaying wood and playing an essential role in breaking down plant material in the ecosystem.

Look-a-like(s): The non-toxic Amber Jelly Roll (*Exidia recisa*) can resemble the Wood Ear but typically exhibits a smaller size and a more translucent appearance and grows on hardwood rather than elder trees.

Cautions: none known.

Culinary Preparation: The Wood Ear's unique texture and mild flavor make it a popular ingredient in various Asian dishes, such as soups and stir-fries. When cooked, it takes on a slightly crunchy, rubbery texture that contrasts your culinary creations. Rinse and soak the dried fungus in water for at least 30 minutes or until it softens and expands.

Medicinal Properties: In traditional Chinese medicine, it has been used to promote circulation, support the immune system, and alleviate respiratory issues. Modern studies suggest that it contains antioxidants and may have potential anti-inflammatory properties.

Fun Fact: The name "Judas's Ear" has biblical origins, as legend has it that Judas Iscariot, the disciple who betrayed Jesus, hanged himself from an elder tree. The Wood Ear's ear-like shape represents Judas's ear, forever eavesdropping on the forest's whispers.

PART EIGHT
THE TIDAL TREASURES
IDENTIFYING COMMON SEAWEEDS

Scan for full color photos

Bladderwrack
Fucus vesiculosus [FYOO-KUS VEH-SIK-YOO-LOH-SUS]

Bladderwrack is a fascinating, nutrient-rich seaweed with a name that might make you giggle. A Fucaceae (wrack) family member, Bladderwrack, goes by other names, such as Rockweed, Black Tang, or Sea Oak.

Location: It's a shoreline superstar, preferring the colder waters of the North Atlantic. You'll find this seaweed rocking the coastlines of North America and Europe, latched onto rocky shores, and flaunting its distinct appearance.

Identification:

GROWTH/SIZE: It can reach lengths of up to 35 inches and is often found in dense, intertidal clusters.

BLADE: Its blades are flat, branching, and olive-green to brownish in color. The small, gas-filled bladders that help the seaweed float closer to the water's surface set Bladderwrack apart.

STIPE: The stipe is short, branching, and tough, connecting the blades to the holdfast.

HOLDFAST: The holdfast is a root-like structure that securely anchors it to rocks and other surfaces in its marine habitat.

Look-a-like(s): Knotted Wrack (*Ascophyllum nodosum*) is a non-toxic look-a-like, but it has a single, long, branching stipe, unlike Bladderwrack's shorter stipe.

Cautions: Always harvest it from clean, uncontaminated waters and wash it thoroughly before consuming. Remember that it is high in iodine, which may cause issues for individuals with thyroid problems.

Culinary Preparation: Bladderwrack is a versatile ingredient enjoyed in soups, salads, or seasoning. Dried and ground into a powder adds a unique umami flavor to your dishes.

Medicinal Properties: Bladderwrack has been traditionally used for its high iodine content, which supports thyroid health. Modern research has discovered its potential benefits for weight loss, digestion, and skin health.

Fun Fact: Bladderwrack was the source of iodine, discovered in 1811, and used to treat goiter, a thyroid gland enlargement.

Dog Toxicity: There is no specific toxicity of Bladderwrack for dogs.

Feather Boa Kelp

Egregia menziesii [EH-GREE-JEE-UH MEN-ZEE-ZEE-EYE]

Feather Boa Kelp is a seaweed that knows how to make an entrance! This attention-grabbing marine plant is part of the Laminariaceae (kelp) family, also known as Sea Palm or Menzies' Egregia.

Location: It can be found strutting its stuff along the Pacific coastlines of North America, from Alaska down to Baja, California. Its preferred habitat is the intertidal and subtidal zones, where it enjoys the ocean's refreshing wave action.

Identification:

GROWTH/SIZE: It can reach impressive lengths of up to 20 feet, making it the life of the underwater party!

BLADE: The seaweed's long, flat, ribbon-like blades are dark brown to olive green and sport numerous, irregularly spaced, fringe-like blades on either side, giving it that iconic feather boa appearance.

Stipe: The stipe is sturdy, branching, and flexible, helping the seaweed withstand the ocean's waves.

Holdfast: The holdfast is a tough, root-like structure that firmly anchors the Feather Boa Kelp to rocks in its marine environment.

Look-a-like(s): It has a unique appearance, so it's not likely to be confused with other seaweeds.

Cautions: it's essential to avoid pulling up the entire plant from the substrate, as this can damage the plant and its surrounding ecosystem. Instead, only the blades should be harvested, leaving the holdfast and stipe intact.

Culinary Preparation: It can be eaten fresh or dried. Use it in salads, stir-fries, or as a wrap for fish or sushi. Its unique texture and mild flavor make it a delicious and nutritious meal addition.

Medicinal Properties: While it does not have specific traditional medicinal uses, seaweeds are known for their rich nutrient content, including vitamins, minerals, and antioxidants that promote overall health.

Fun Fact: Feather Boa Kelp is a favorite among marine life, providing food and shelter to various species. Its holdfast also acts as a nursery for smaller organisms, such as sea snails and crabs.

Dog Toxicity: Feather Boa Kelp has no specific toxicity for dogs.

Green Caviar
Caulerpa lentillifera [KAW-ler-puh len-tuh-LIF-er-uh]

Green Caviar is the jewel of the sea. Belonging to the Caulerpaceae (sea lettuce) family, this luxurious seaweed is known by other captivating names, such as Sea Grapes or Umibudo.

Location: It prefers the finer things in life, enjoying the warm, shallow waters of the tropical Indo-Pacific region. It's commonly found in the coastal areas of Japan, the Philippines, Vietnam, and Indonesia.

Identification:

GROWTH/SIZE: Green Caviar grows in clusters of small, round, translucent green beads that resemble caviar, reaching lengths of 2-5 inches.

BLADE: Unlike other seaweeds, Green Caviar doesn't have a traditional blade. Instead, it boasts a unique bead-like appearance, contributing to its luxurious status.

Stipe: The stipe is slender, creeping, and branched, allowing it to spread across the seafloor.

Holdfast: The holdfast is a small, disc-like structure that secures it to substrates such as rocks, coral, or even sandy bottoms.

Look-a-like(s): While it's quite distinctive, it may be confused with other members of the Caulerpa family. However, its bead-like appearance sets it apart from its relatives.

Cautions: Seaweed can harbor bacteria such as Vibrio species that can cause illness, especially if consumed raw seaweed.

Culinary Preparation: It's enjoyed fresh in salads, as a garnish, or as a snack with a dipping sauce. Its unique texture and salty flavor add a touch of elegance to any dish.

Medicinal Properties: Traditionally, Green Caviar is valued for its high nutrient content, including vitamins, minerals, and antioxidants. Modern research has shown that it may help reduce blood sugar levels and support heart health.

Fun Fact: In Japan, Green Caviar is considered a delicacy and a symbol of good luck, often served during special occasions and celebrations.

Dog Toxicity: There is no specific toxicity of Green Caviar for dogs.

Irish Moss
Chondrus crispus [KON-DRUS KRIS-PUS]

Irish Moss is a red seaweed from the Gigartinaceae (giant kelp) family. It goes by a few other names, such as Carrageen Moss or simply Carrageen, giving the nod to its Irish heritage.

Location: It's a fan of the cool waters in the North Atlantic Ocean. It can flourish on rocky coastlines from Canada to Europe, particularly in Ireland, where it's a beloved local treasure.

Identification:

GROWTH/SIZE: This fan-shaped seaweed grows 2-7 inches tall, showcasing a lush, emerald hue that would make any leprechaun green with envy.

BLADE: The blades are thin and flat, forming branching, fan-like segments.

STIPE: The stipe is short and inconspicuous, which allows the blades to take center stage.

Holdfast: It clings to rocks and other submerged surfaces using a small, disc-like holdfast that keeps it anchored.

Look-a-like(s): It can be mistaken for other red seaweeds, such as Star Moss (*Mastocarpus stellatus*). However, it can be distinguished by its slippery texture and the absence of visible reproductive structures.

Cautions: It contains carrageenan, a compound that can cause digestive upset or irritation in some individuals when consumed in large amounts.

Culinary Preparation: Irish Moss is a natural thickening agent, perfect for puddings, sauces, and soups. It also serves as a vegan gelatin alternative and adds a smooth texture to smoothies and ice cream.

Medicinal Properties: Traditionally, Irish Moss was used to soothe respiratory issues, such as coughs and sore throats. Modern research suggests it may support digestive health and boost the immune system thanks to its rich nutrient profile.

Fun Fact: During the Irish Potato Famine in the 1800s, Irish Moss was a vital source of nutrition, saving countless lives with its rich array of vitamins and minerals.

Dog Toxicity: There's no specific toxicity associated with Irish Moss for dogs.

Oarweed
Laminaria digitata [LAH-MUH-NAIR-EE-UH DIH-JIH-TAH-TUH]

Oarweed is a captivating brown seaweed in the Laminariaceae (kelp) family. This nautical gem has a few other names, such as Tangleweed, Fingered Tangle, and Sea Girdles, which perfectly capture its maritime charm.

Location: It thrives in the cool waters of the North Atlantic Ocean, clinging to rocky shorelines from the Arctic regions down to the coasts of Europe and the northeastern United States. These kelp forests provide a haven for marine life, creating a thriving underwater community.

Identification:

GROWTH/SIZE: It can grow quite large, reaching lengths of up to 6.5-10 feet with a width of 1-2 inches.

BLADE: This seaweed features long, strap-like blades divided into multiple finger-like segments, resembling the oars of a ship.

STIPE: The stipe is long, cylindrical, and flexible, allowing Oarweed to sway gracefully with the ocean currents.

HOLDFAST: A claw-like holdfast anchors it to rocky surfaces, ensuring it remains secure even in the roughest seas.

Look-a-like(s): It can be mistaken for other kelp species, such as Sugar Kelp (*Saccharina latissima*) or Furbelows (*Saccorhiza polyschides*), but its distinct finger-like blade segments set it apart.

Cautions: Consuming large amounts can cause digestive discomfort, including bloating, gas, and diarrhea.

Culinary Preparation: It can be enjoyed in various dishes, such as soups, salads, and stir-fries. Its rich, umami flavor adds depth to any culinary creation, and its high iodine content makes it a nutritious addition to the plate.

Medicinal Properties: Historically, it was used to treat goiter and other iodine-deficiency-related disorders. Today, its potential health benefits include supporting thyroid function and providing essential minerals for overall well-being.

Fun Fact: The Vikings were known to use Oarweed to create a type of soda ash, which was a crucial component in producing glass and soap.

Dog Toxicity: There's no known toxicity associated with Oarweed for dogs.

Sea Belt
Saccharina latissima [SUH-KAR-EE-NUH LUH-TIS-UH-MUH]

Seat Belt is a brown seaweed from the Laminariaceae (kelp) family. Also known as Sugar Kelp or Sweet Kombu, this stylish seaweed has an alluring sweetness that distinguishes it from other marine flora.

Location: Sea Belt's preferred runway is the cold, rocky shorelines of the North Atlantic Ocean, stretching from the Arctic down to the North Sea and the northeastern coasts of the United States. This elegant seaweed adorns the underwater world, creating an excellent environment for marine life.

Identification:

GROWTH/SIZE: It can grow to an impressive 10-16 feet in length and 4-8 inches in width.

BLADE: The blade is long, undivided, and wavy, resembling a delicate and fashionable belt.

Stipe: The stipe is short, narrow, and cylindrical, connecting the blade to the holdfast.

Holdfast: The holdfast is a hapteron, a root-like structure that grips onto rocks and other underwater surfaces.

Look-a-like(s): Sea Belt might be mistaken for Oarweed (*Laminaria digitata*) or Furbelows (*Saccorhiza polyschides*). Still, its wavy, undivided blade sets it apart from the rest of the kelp crowd.

Cautions: Over-harvesting sugar kelp can negatively impact the marine ecosystem. It's important to follow sustainable harvesting practices and not to harvest more than necessary. Check local regulations and guidelines for sustainable seaweed harvesting practices.

Culinary Preparation: Sea Belt's slightly sweet flavor and silky texture make it a versatile ingredient in the kitchen. Use it in soups, salads, sushi rolls, or as a delicious wrap for steamed fish or vegetables.

Medicinal Properties: Traditionally, Sea Belt was used for its high iodine content, which can help support thyroid health. Modern research suggests it may also provide anti-inflammatory and antioxidant benefits.

Fun Fact: Sea Belt's natural sweetness comes from the sugar-like molecule, mannitol, which is extracted and used as a sugar substitute for people with diabetes and those looking to reduce their sugar intake.

Dog Toxicity: Sea Belt is not known to be toxic to dogs.

Sea Colander
Agarum cribrosum [UH-GAIR-UHM KRIH-BROH-SUHM]

Sea Colander is a part of the Phaeophyceae (brown algae) family. Also known as Agarum, this lovely seaweed flaunts a unique net-like structure, making it the darling of the underwater world.

Location: It graces the subtidal zones of the cold North Atlantic Ocean, specifically around the coasts of Greenland, Iceland, and eastern Canada. Its beautiful lattice design provides shelter and habitat for various marine critters.

Identification:

GROWTH/SIZE: Sea Colander can reach up to 3 feet long, with a wide, fan-like blade.

BLADE: The most striking feature of the Sea Colander is its delicate, reticulated blade, resembling a lacy colander.

Stipe: The stipe is short and cylindrical, serving as the foundation for the beautiful net-like blade.

Holdfast: The holdfast is a hapteron, gripping tightly onto rocks and other underwater surfaces.

Look-a-like(s): While its unique appearance sets it apart, Sea Colander could potentially be confused with other brown seaweeds, such as Sugar Kelp (*Saccharina latissima*) or Furbelows (*Saccorhiza polyschides*). However, the distinct lattice pattern of the Sea Colander makes it easily distinguishable.

Cautions: When harvesting giant kelp, be aware of the surrounding environment, including the tides and surf conditions. Use appropriate safety gear, such as wetsuits and flotation devices, and avoid areas with strong currents or rough waves.

Culinary Preparation: Sea Colander's intriguing texture and mild flavor make it perfect for soups, salads, and wraps. It can also be dried and ground into a fine powder for a thickening agent in various dishes.

Medicinal Properties: Although not well-known for its medicinal properties, Sea Colander is a rich source of essential minerals like iodine and potassium, which may support thyroid health and overall well-being.

Fun Fact: Sea Colander's unique net-like structure has inspired many artists and designers, who have incorporated its delicate pattern into various forms of art and fashion.

Dog Toxicity: No known reports of Sea Colander being toxic to dogs.

Sea Lettuce
Ulva lactuca [UL-vuh lak-TOO-kuh]

Sea Lettuce is a bright green, edible seaweed making waves in the culinary world. This aquatic plant also goes by the name Green Laver or Green Seaweed, as part of the Ulvaceae (sea lettuce) family.

Location: It's a seaweed found in intertidal zones and shallow waters near rocky coastlines worldwide. From the shores of Europe to North America, Asia, and Oceania coastlines, you'll spot this vibrant green beauty waving hello.

Identification:

GROWTH/SIZE: It forms thin, delicate, and translucent blades up to 10 inches long.

BLADE: The blade is characterized by its bright green color, ruffled edges, and flat, lettuce-like appearance. It's composed of two cell layers, making it incredibly thin.

Stipe: This seaweed lacks a distinct stipe, as the blade connects directly to the holdfast.

Holdfast: The holdfast is a small, root-like structure that anchors to rocks, shells, or other hard surfaces in its marine environment.

Look-a-like(s): Some non-toxic seaweed species, such as Linnaeus Sea Lettuce (*Ulva linza*) and Green Sea Lettuce (*Ulva prolifera*), resemble Sea Lettuce but are often smaller in size and have distinct variations in blade shape.

Cautions: Avoid areas with potential pollution or contaminated waters when foraging for Sea Lettuce. Always clean the seaweed thoroughly before consumption.

Culinary Preparation: Sea Lettuce is a versatile ingredient that can be eaten raw, blanched, or dried. Its mild, slightly salty flavor makes it an excellent addition to salads, wraps, sushi, or as a crunchy, nutritious snack when dehydrated.

Medicinal Properties: Traditionally, Sea Lettuce has been consumed for its high mineral content, including iodine, iron, and magnesium. It's also a good source of vitamins A, B, and C and contains protein and dietary fiber.

Fun Fact: In the 17th century, famed English diarist Samuel Pepys wrote about eating "Laver," a dish made from Sea Lettuce, demonstrating its culinary use even centuries ago.

Dog Toxicity: There is no known toxicity of Sea Lettuce for dogs.

Winged Kelp
Alaria marginata [UH-LAIR-EE-UH MAR-JIN-AH-TUH]

Winged Kelp is an edible seaweed that's been tickling taste buds and intriguing botanists for centuries. Part of the Alariaceae (brown algae) family, the Winged Kelp is also known by names like Atlantic Wakame, Dabberlocks, and Murlins.

Location: You'll find Winged Kelp riding the waves in cold, temperate waters of the North Atlantic, particularly along the rocky shores of Europe and the east coast of North America. Just look for the fascinating, winged structures swaying gracefully underwater.

Identification:

GROWTH/SIZE: Winged Kelp is an impressive seaweed that can reach up to 10 feet long.

BLADE: The main feature of the Winged Kelp is its narrow, ribbon-like blade with its "wings," or lateral blades, which run along its length. The color varies from dark brown to greenish-brown.

Stipe: Winged Kelp has a short, flexible stipe that connects the blade to the holdfast.

Holdfast: The holdfast is a claw-like structure that securely attaches the seaweed to rocks or other surfaces in its marine habitat.

Look-a-like(s): Sugar Kelp (*Saccharina latissima*) is a non-toxic look-a-like, but it lacks the distinctive lateral blades or "wings" of Winged Kelp.

Cautions: When harvesting Winged Kelp, choose clean, unpolluted waters and wash the seaweed thoroughly before consumption.

Culinary Preparation: Winged Kelp is a culinary delight, whether raw, cooked, or dried. Its slightly sweet and nutty flavor makes it a fantastic addition to salads, soups, or stir-fries.

Medicinal Properties: Historically, Winged Kelp has been valued for its high mineral and vitamin content, including iodine, calcium, and vitamins A, B, and C. It's also a source of dietary fiber and antioxidants.

Fun Fact: Seaweed has been consumed in Iceland and other Nordic countries for centuries, often used as a traditional ingredient in soups and stews.

Dog Toxicity: There is no known toxicity of Winged Kelp for dogs.

PART NINE
LOOK, BUT DON'T TASTE
IDENTIFYING HAZARDOUS FOLIAGE AND FUNGI

Scan for full color photos

BLACK HENBANE

Hyoscyamus niger [HYE-OH-SY-UH-MUHS NYE-JER]

All parts of the plant are toxic, but the seeds and leaves contain the highest concentration of poisonous alkaloids, including hyoscyamine and scopolamine. These chemicals can cause various symptoms, including hallucinations, delirium, blurred vision, dilated pupils, dry mouth, and even death in severe cases. Signs of Black Henbane poisoning can appear within 30 minutes to a few hours of ingestion, and the severity of the symptoms will depend on the amount consumed.

Black Henbane can be easily confused with other non-toxic plants such as mullein, mint, and foxglove. Its leaves are large and toothed, similar to tobacco, but with a more pointed shape. The flowers are bell-shaped and yellow with purple veins resembling the morning glory.

DEADLY GALERINA

Galerina autumnalis [GUH-LAIR-IN-UH AW-TUH-NAHL-IS]

One of the most dangerous aspects is that it closely resembles several edible mushroom species, such as honey mushrooms and shiitake mushrooms. Poisoning symptoms can take hours or even days, including nausea, vomiting, abdominal pain, and diarrhea. As the poisoning progresses, it can cause liver damage and lead to liver failure, which can be fatal. Treatment may involve inducing vomiting, administering activated charcoal to absorb the toxins or even a liver transplant in severe cases.

FLY AGARIC

Amanita muscaria [UH-MAN-IH-TUH MUH-SKAIR-EE-UH]

A strikingly beautiful mushroom with a bright red cap speckled with white spots. Although it has a long history of use in shamanic and cultural practices, it is also one of the most toxic mushrooms in the world. One of the biggest risks is its resemblance to edible mushrooms, such as the straw mushroom and the shaggy mane. These look-alike mushrooms grow in similar habitats and have similar characteristics, making them easy to confuse. If you suspect someone has consumed Amanita muscaria, it is important to seek medical attention immediately. The toxins can cause various symptoms, from nausea and vomiting to delirium, seizures, and coma. In severe cases, it can be fatal. Symptoms may not appear for several hours after ingestion, but early treatment can be critical for a successful recovery. Symptoms of poisoning may include abdominal pain, nausea, vomiting, diarrhea, sweating, dizziness, confusion, and hallucinations.

JIMSONWEED

Datura stramonium [DUH-TOO-RUH STRUH-MOH-NEE-UH]

Jimsonweed is a highly toxic and hallucinogenic plant native to North America but has since been introduced to other regions worldwide. This plant can grow up to 5 feet tall and is easily recognizable by its large, trumpet-shaped white or pale purple flowers and spiky, egg-shaped seed pods containing numerous tiny black seeds. It's common in fields, waste places, and roadsides and is considered invasive in many areas. All parts of the plant, including the leaves, seeds, and flowers, contain toxic compounds such as atropine, scopolamine, and hyoscyamine, which can cause hallucinations, delirium, tachycardia, and respiratory depression. Ingesting even a small amount of this plant can be fatal, making avoiding contact with or ingestion essential.

GREY KNIGHT

Tricholoma terreum [TRICK-OH-LOH-MUH EH-KWES-TREE]

One of the main concerns with the grey knight is its potential toxicity. While eating when cooked is generally considered safe, some individuals may experience adverse reactions. Symptoms of poisoning can include gastrointestinal distress, vomiting, diarrhea, and in severe cases, liver or kidney damage. Another challenge when foraging for the grey knight is identifying it correctly. It  can easily be mistaken for other mushrooms, such as the deadly galerina or the poisonous green-spored lepiota. Despite these challenges, the grey knight remains a beloved and sought-after ingredient for many mushroom enthusiasts. It can be found in various habitats, including mixed forests and woodlands, and is often abundant in late summer and early fall.

SNOWDROP

Galanthus nivalis [GUH-LAN-THUS NYE-VAL-IS]

The plant contains the toxin galantamine, which can cause various symptoms, including nausea, vomiting, diarrhea, and in severe cases, convulsions, and coma. It is also toxic to pets and livestock and can cause similar symptoms.

It is essential to identify snowdrops to avoid confusion with other plants that may look similar. Snowdrops have long, narrow leaves that emerge directly from the ground and a single, white, drooping flower with three petals and a green ovary. The flower has a distinct shape and is easily recognizable once seen.

There are a few plants that resemble snowdrops but are not toxic. These include the autumn snowflake and the spring snowflake, which have similar flowers but bloom later in the season. It is essential to correctly identify any wild plant before consuming it, as misidentification can lead to severe illness or even death.

THE SICKENER

R*ussula emetica [ROO-SUH-LUH EH-MET-IH-KUH]*
This highly toxic mushroom is bright red and has a distinctive cap with a convex shape that can reach up to 10 cm in diameter. Despite its attractive appearance, consuming even a small amount of this mushroom can cause severe poisoning. Poisoning symptoms typically begin within 30 minutes to 2 hours after consumption and can include intense stomach cramps, vomiting, and  diarrhea. These symptoms can last for several hours and may require hospitalization. In severe cases, respiratory distress and shock can occur, which can be life-threatening. It is important to note that Russula emetica has several edible look-a-like species, including Russula rosacea and Russula nobilis. These mushrooms are similar in appearance but lack a distinctive spicy taste and a pungent odor.

WESTERN YEW

Taxus brevifolia [TAK-SUS BREV-IH-FOH-LEE-UH]

All parts of the Pacific yew tree, except for the fleshy red aril around the seed, contain the toxic compound taxine. The severity of poisoning from Pacific yew consumption varies, but symptoms can include nausea, vomiting, dizziness, tremors, seizures, and heart failure. One of the biggest concerns with Pacific yew is its similarity to other edible yew species. While Pacific yew has shorter needles and red arils, other yew species, such as the English yew, can be mistaken for it. The English yew is also toxic, but its arils are not edible, making it even more dangerous. Because of its toxicity, Pacific yew is not typically used in culinary preparations. However, the plant has been studied for its medicinal properties, and a chemotherapy drug called paclitaxel is derived from the bark of the Pacific yew tree.

DEVIL'S CLUB

O*plopanax horridus [uh-PLOP-uh-naks HORE-ih-dus]*

While Devil's Club can be a valuable plant for traditional medicine, it should be handled cautiously. The plant is known to be toxic if ingested, and its sap and thorns can cause skin irritation and pain. Wearing protective clothing and gloves when handling Devil's Club is important.

It is crucial to correctly identify Devil's Club to avoid accidentally consuming toxic look-a-like plants such as elderberry or American ginseng. Devil's Club poisoning symptoms include nausea, vomiting, diarrhea, and stomach pain. If ingested, it is important to seek medical attention immediately.

PART TEN
WILDLY DELICIOUS
20 RECIPES FOR COOKING WITH EDIBLE PLANTS FROM NATURE

Blackcap Raspberry Preserves

Ingredients:

- 4 cups fresh Blackcap raspberries
- 2 cups granulated sugar
- 1 tablespoon lemon juice
- 1/2 teaspoon butter (optional, to reduce foaming)
- 1 packet (1.75 ounces) of regular powdered fruit pectin

Instructions:

1. Prepare jars and lids: Sterilize jars and lids by boiling them in a large pot of water for at least 10 minutes. Keep the jars warm in the hot water until ready to use.
2. In a large saucepan, combine Blackcap raspberries and lemon juice. Stir in pectin until dissolved.
3. Bring the mixture to a full rolling boil over high heat, stirring constantly to prevent sticking.
4. Add sugar and butter (if using) to the saucepan. Return to a full rolling boil and continue boiling for exactly 1 minute, stirring constantly.
5. Remove from heat and skim off any foam with a metal spoon.
6. Ladle hot preserves into hot sterilized jars, leaving 1/4-inch headspace. Wipe the jar rims clean with a damp cloth to ensure a proper seal.
7. Place lids and screw bands on the jars, tightening until finger-tight. Do not over tighten.
8. Process jars in a water bath canner for 10 minutes (adjusting the processing time for your altitude if necessary).
9. Remove jars from the canner using a jar lifter and let them cool on a wire rack, undisturbed, for at least 12 hours.
10. Check the seals by pressing the center of each lid. If it does not pop back, the jar is properly sealed. If the lid pops back, refrigerate the jar and use the preserves within a few weeks.

Enjoy your homemade Blackcap Raspberry Preserves on toast, biscuits, or in your favorite dessert recipes! Store sealed jars in a cool, dark place for up to one year. Refrigerate after opening.

Ocean Spray Berry Tart with Almond Crust

Servings: 8

Prep Time: 1 hour 30 minutes (including chilling time)

Ingredients:

For the Almond Crust:

- 1 cup all-purpose flour
- 1/2 cup almond flour
- 1/4 cup granulated sugar
- 1/4 teaspoon salt
- 1/2 cup cold unsalted butter, cubed
- 1 large egg yolk
- 2 tablespoons ice water

For the Ocean Spray Berry Filling:

- 2 cups fresh Ocean Spray berries, cleaned and dried
- 1/2 cup granulated sugar
- 1 tablespoon cornstarch
- 1 tablespoon lemon juice
- 1/4 teaspoon ground cinnamon

Instructions:

1. In a food processor, combine all-purpose flour, almond flour, sugar, and salt. Pulse a few times to mix.
2. Add the cold cubed butter to the food processor and pulse until the mixture resembles coarse crumbs.
3. In a small bowl, whisk together the egg yolk and ice water. Add this mixture to the food processor and pulse until the dough comes together.
4. Turn the dough out onto a lightly floured surface and shape it into a disc. Wrap the dough in plastic wrap and refrigerate for 30 minutes.
5. Preheat the oven to 375°F (190°C).
6. Roll out the chilled dough on a lightly floured surface into a 12-inch circle. Carefully transfer the dough to a 9-inch tart pan with a removable bottom, pressing it into the bottom and up the sides of the pan. Trim off any excess dough.

7. Prick the bottom of the crust with a fork, then line the crust with parchment paper and fill it with pie weights or dried beans. Bake for 20 minutes.
8. Remove the parchment paper and weights, then bake the crust for another 10-12 minutes, or until golden brown. Allow the crust to cool completely on a wire rack.
9. In a medium saucepan, combine the Ocean Spray berries, sugar, cornstarch, lemon juice, and cinnamon. Cook over medium heat, stirring occasionally, until the mixture thickens and the berries release their juices, about 5-7 minutes. Remove from heat and let the filling cool slightly.
10. Pour the Ocean Spray berry filling into the cooled almond crust, spreading it evenly.
11. Refrigerate the tart for at least 30 minutes to allow the filling to set.

Serve the Ocean Spray Berry Tart chilled or at room temperature, garnished with whipped cream or a scoop of vanilla ice cream. Enjoy!

Oregon Cherry Clafoutis

yields 4-6 servings

Prep time: 10 minutes

Bake time: 30-35 minutes

Ingredients:

- 1 cup fresh Oregon cherries, pitted
- 1/2 cup all-purpose flour
- 1/4 cup granulated sugar
- 1/4 tsp salt
- 3 large eggs
- 1 cup milk
- 1 tsp vanilla extract
- Powdered sugar for garnish

Instructions:

1. Preheat the oven to 375°F (190°C).
2. Grease a 9-inch baking dish with butter or cooking spray.
3. Arrange the pitted cherries in a single layer at the bottom of the baking dish.
4. Whisk together flour, sugar, and salt in a medium mixing bowl.
5. In a separate bowl, beat the eggs until light and fluffy.
6. Slowly whisk in the milk and vanilla extract until well combined.
7. Add the dry ingredients to the wet ingredients and whisk until smooth.
8. Pour the batter over the cherries in the baking dish.
9. Bake for 30-35 minutes or until the clafoutis is set and golden brown.
10. Allow to cool for 10-15 minutes before dusting with powdered sugar and serving.

Enjoy!

Oregon Grape Mead

Servings: This recipe yields approximately 1 gallon of mead

Prep Time: Approximately 1 hour, not including fermentation and aging time.

Ingredients:

- 3 lbs of honey
- 1 lb Oregon grape berries
- 1-gallon water
- 1 packet of champagne yeast
- 1 tsp yeast nutrient

Instructions:

1. Crush the Oregon grape berries and place them in a large pot with the water. Bring to a boil and simmer for 15 minutes. Turn off the heat and let it cool to room temperature.
2. Strain the liquid through a fine mesh strainer or cheesecloth to remove any pulp or seeds. Discard solids.
3. Add honey and yeast nutrients to the strained liquid and stir until dissolved.
4. Pour the mixture into a sanitized fermenting vessel and add the packet of champagne yeast.
5. Cover the vessel with an airlock and let it ferment for 2-3 weeks, or until fermentation has stopped.
6. Once fermentation has stopped, rack the mead into a sanitized secondary fermenting vessel and let it age for several months, or until it has reached the desired flavor and clarity.
7. Bottle and store in a cool, dark place until ready to serve.

Salal Berry & Apple Crisp

Servings: 6

Prep Time: 20 minutes - Cook Time: 45 minutes

Ingredients:

- 2 cups fresh Salal berries, rinsed and drained
- 2 cups peeled, cored, and sliced apples (about 2-3 medium apples)
- 1 tablespoon lemon juice
- 1/2 cup granulated sugar
- 1 teaspoon ground cinnamon
- 1/2 teaspoon ground nutmeg
- 1 cup all-purpose flour
- 1/2 cup packed brown sugar
- 1/2 cup rolled oats
- 1/2 cup cold unsalted butter, cubed
- 1/4 teaspoon salt

Instructions:

1. Preheat your oven to 350°F (175°C). Lightly grease a 9-inch square baking dish.
2. In a large mixing bowl, combine Salal berries, sliced apples, and lemon juice. Toss gently to coat the fruit evenly with lemon juice.
3. In a separate small bowl, mix together granulated sugar, cinnamon, and nutmeg. Sprinkle the sugar mixture over the fruit and toss gently to coat.
4. Transfer the fruit mixture to the prepared baking dish, spreading it out evenly.
5. In another mixing bowl, combine flour, brown sugar, rolled oats, and salt. Add cold, cubed butter and use a pastry cutter or your fingers to work the butter into the dry ingredients until the mixture resembles coarse crumbs.
6. Sprinkle the crumb mixture evenly over the fruit layer in the baking dish.
7. Bake in the preheated oven for 45 minutes, or until the topping is golden brown and the fruit is bubbling.
8. Remove from the oven and let cool slightly before serving.

Serve your Salal Berry & Apple Crisp warm with a scoop of vanilla ice cream or a dollop of whipped cream. Enjoy!

Fireweed Honey Butter

Servings: 8

Prep time: 10 minutes

Ingredients:

- 1/2 cup unsalted butter, at room temperature
- 2 tbsp Fireweed honey
- 1 tbsp finely chopped fresh Fireweed leaves

Instructions:

1. In a mixing bowl, beat the butter until creamy.
2. Add the Fireweed honey and beat until well combined.
3. Add the chopped Fireweed leaves and beat until evenly distributed throughout the butter.
4. Transfer the Fireweed honey butter to a serving dish or jar.
5. Chill the Fireweed honey butter for at least 30 minutes before serving to allow the flavors to meld together.
6. Serve the Fireweed honey butter with your favorite bread or baked goods, such as muffins, scones, or biscuits.

Enjoy the unique taste of Fireweed in this delicious spread!

Licorice Root Tea

Servings: 4 cups of tea

Prep Time: 5 minutes

Cook Time: 15 minutes

Ingredients:

- 1 tablespoon dried licorice root
- 4 cups water
- honey (optional)
- lemon (optional)

Instructions:

1. Bring 4 cups of water to a boil in a pot.
2. Add 1 tablespoon of dried licorice root to the boiling water.
3. Reduce the heat and let the mixture simmer for 10-15 minutes.
4. Remove the pot from the heat and let it cool for 5 minutes.
5. Strain the tea into a cup or teapot.
6. Add honey or lemon to taste, if desired.

Serve and enjoy!

Yerba Buena Iced Tea

Servings: 4

Prep time: 10 minutes

Ingredients:

- 4 cups of water
- 1/2 cup of fresh Yerba Buena leaves, lightly packed
- 1/4 cup of honey
- Juice of 2 limes
- Lime slices, for garnish
- Ice cubes

Instructions:

1. In a saucepan, bring the water to a boil.
2. Add the Yerba Buena leaves and reduce heat to low. Let the leaves steep for 5-7 minutes.
3. Strain the mixture into a pitcher and discard the leaves.
4. Stir in honey and lime juice until fully combined.
5. Chill the tea in the refrigerator for at least 1 hour.
6. When ready to serve, add ice cubes to a glass and pour the tea over the ice.
7. Garnish with lime slices and serve.

Enjoy this refreshing Yerba Buena iced tea on a hot summer day!

Golden Western Salsify Hash

Serves 4

Prep time: 45 minutes

Ingredients:

- 1 lb Western Salsify roots
- 1/2 cup all-purpose flour
- 2 tbsp olive oil
- 2 cloves garlic, minced
- 1/4 tsp red pepper flakes
- 1/4 tsp salt
- 1/4 tsp black pepper
- 2 cups vegetable broth
- 2 tbsp chopped fresh parsley
- Lemon wedges, for serving

Instructions:

1. Wash the Western Salsify roots thoroughly and peel them with a vegetable peeler. Cut them into 2-inch pieces and soak them in cold water with a splash of vinegar for 10 minutes.
2. Drain the salsify pieces and pat them dry with paper towels. Roll them in flour until evenly coated.
3. Heat the olive oil in a large skillet over medium-high heat. Add the garlic, red pepper flakes, salt, and black pepper, and stir until fragrant.
4. Add the floured salsify pieces to the skillet and cook for about 5 minutes, or until lightly browned on all sides.
5. Pour the vegetable broth over the salsify and bring to a simmer. Cover the skillet and cook for 20-25 minutes, or until the salsify is tender.
6. Remove the skillet from the heat and stir in the chopped parsley.
7. Serve the Western Salsify hot with lemon wedges on the side.

Enjoy your delicious and nutritious Western Salsify dish!

Roasted Beaked Hazelnuts

serves 4-6 people:

Prep time: 5 minutes

Cook time: 15 minutes

Ingredients:

- 2 cups of fresh beaked hazelnuts
- 1 tablespoon of olive oil
- 1 teaspoon of sea salt
- Optional: additional spices like smoked paprika or chili powder

Instructions:

1. Preheat your oven to 350°F (175°C).
2. Place the beaked hazelnuts in a single layer on a baking sheet.
3. Drizzle the olive oil over the hazelnuts and sprinkle with sea salt (and any additional spices, if desired).
4. Use your hands to toss the hazelnuts to ensure they are evenly coated in oil and spices.
5. Roast the hazelnuts in the oven for about 15 minutes, or until they are lightly golden and fragrant.
6. Remove the baking sheet from the oven and let the hazelnuts cool for a few minutes before serving.

These roasted beaked hazelnuts make a delicious and healthy snack that's perfect for any time of day. Enjoy!

Pacific Crabapple Sauce

Servings: 4-6

Prep Time: 20 minutes

Ingredients:

- 4 cups Pacific Crabapples, washed and cored
- 1 cup water
- 1/2 cup sugar
- 1 cinnamon stick
- 1 tsp vanilla extract

Instructions:

1. In a medium saucepan, combine the Pacific Crabapples, water, sugar, and cinnamon stick.
2. Cook over medium heat, stirring occasionally, until the crabapples are tender and the liquid has thickened slightly about 15-20 minutes.
3. Remove the cinnamon stick and stir in the vanilla extract.
4. Using an immersion blender or a food processor, puree the mixture until smooth.
5. Let the sauce cool to room temperature, then store in an airtight container in the refrigerator for up to 1 week.
6. Serve as a topping for pancakes, waffles, oatmeal, or ice cream, or use it as a condiment for pork or chicken dishes.

Enjoy your delicious and flavorful Pacific Crabapple sauce!

Western Chokecherry Jelly

Servings: 8 cups of jelly

Prep time: approximately 2 hours.

Ingredients:

- 6 cups chokecherries
- 6 cups water
- 1 package (1.75 oz) of powdered pectin
- 7 cups sugar

Instructions:

1. Rinse and drain the chokecherries.
2. In a large pot, add the chokecherries and water, and bring to a boil. Reduce heat and simmer for 30 minutes.
3. Strain the juice through a jelly bag or cheesecloth, and discard the pulp.
4. Measure 4 cups of chokecherry juice into a large pot.
5. Add the powdered pectin to the juice, and stir until dissolved.
6. Bring the mixture to a rolling boil over high heat, stirring constantly.
7. Add the sugar, and continue stirring until it dissolves. Bring the mixture back to a rolling boil.
8. Boil for 1 minute, stirring constantly.
9. Remove from heat and skim off any foam.
10. Pour the hot jelly into sterilized jars, leaving 1/4 inch headspace.
11. Wipe the rims and threads of the jars with a clean, damp cloth, and screw on the lids.
12. Process the jars in a boiling water bath for 10 minutes.
13. Remove from the water bath and let cool on a towel-lined countertop.
14. Store in a cool, dry place.

Candy Cap Cookies

Servings: 20-24 cookies

Prep Time: 20 minutes

Bake Time: 10-12 minutes

Ingredients:

- 1/2 cup unsalted butter, softened
- 1/2 cup granulated sugar
- 1/2 cup brown sugar
- 1 egg
- 1 tsp vanilla extract
- 2 cups all-purpose flour
- 1 tsp baking soda
- 1/2 tsp salt
- 1/2 cup dried Candy Cap mushrooms, finely ground in a food processor or coffee grinder

Directions:

1. Preheat the oven to 375°F. Line a baking sheet with parchment paper.
2. In a large mixing bowl, cream together the butter, granulated sugar, and brown sugar until light and fluffy.
3. Beat in the egg and vanilla extract until well combined.
4. In a separate mixing bowl, whisk together the flour, baking soda, salt, and ground Candy Cap mushrooms.
5. Gradually add the dry ingredients to the wet ingredients, mixing until well combined.
6. Roll the dough into small balls (about 1 tablespoon each) and place them onto the prepared baking sheet, leaving about 2 inches of space between each cookie.
7. Bake for 10-12 minutes, or until the cookies are lightly golden brown on the edges.
8. Remove from the oven and let cool on the baking sheet for 5 minutes before transferring to a wire rack to cool completely.

Enjoy your delicious and unique Candy Cap cookies!

Coral Tooth Delight

Serves 4 people

Prep time: approximately 30 minutes

Ingredients:

- 1 lb Coral Tooth Fungus
- 2 tbsp olive oil
- 2 garlic cloves, minced
- 1/4 tsp red pepper flakes
- Salt and pepper to taste

Instructions:

1. Clean the Coral Tooth Fungus by gently brushing off any dirt or debris. Rinse with cool water and pat dry with paper towels.
2. Cut the fungus into bite-sized pieces and set aside.
3. In a large skillet, heat the olive oil over medium heat.
4. Add the garlic and red pepper flakes, and cook for about 1 minute or until fragrant.
5. Add the Coral Tooth Fungus to the skillet and stir to coat with the garlic and oil mixture.
6. Cook for about 5-7 minutes, stirring occasionally, or until the fungus is tender and lightly browned.
7. Season with salt and pepper to taste.
8. Serve hot as a side dish or use it as a topping for pizza, pasta, or rice.

Enjoy your Coral Tooth Fungus dish!

Reishi Tea

Servings: 4 cups

Prep time: 5 minutes

Cook time: 2-3 hours

Ingredients:

- 2-3 grams of dried Reishi mushroom slices
- 4 cups of water
- Optional additions: honey, lemon, ginger

Instructions:

1. Bring the water to a boil in a medium-sized pot.
2. Add the Reishi mushroom slices to the pot and reduce the heat to low.
3. Let the Reishi simmer for about 2-3 hours.
4. Remove the pot from the heat and let it cool for a few minutes.
5. Strain the tea through a fine-mesh sieve or cheesecloth to remove any mushroom pieces.
6. Add honey, lemon, or ginger to taste, if desired.
7. Serve hot or chilled.

Sautéed Western Yellowfoot Mushrooms

Servings: 4

Prep Time: 10 minutes

Cook Time: 15 minutes

Ingredients:

- 1 pound fresh Western Yellowfoot mushrooms
- 2 tablespoons olive oil
- 2 cloves garlic, minced
- Salt and pepper to taste
- 1 tablespoon chopped fresh parsley (optional)

Instructions:

1. Clean the Western Yellowfoot mushrooms by brushing off any dirt with a soft-bristled brush or damp paper towel. Trim the stem ends and discard any tough or discolored parts.
2. Heat the olive oil in a large skillet over medium heat. Add the minced garlic and sauté for about 1 minute until fragrant.
3. Add the Western Yellowfoot mushrooms to the skillet and sauté for 10-12 minutes until tender and lightly browned. Stir occasionally.
4. Season with salt and pepper to taste. Garnish with chopped fresh parsley if desired.
5. Serve the sautéed Western Yellowfoot mushrooms as a side dish or add them to omelets, pasta dishes, or pizzas.

Enjoy your delicious and healthy Western Yellowfoot mushrooms!

Wood Ear Salad

Serves 4

Prep Time: 15 minutes

Ingredients:

- 2 cups of fresh Wood Ear mushrooms
- 1/4 cup of thinly sliced scallions
- 2 cloves of garlic, minced
- 1 tbsp of soy sauce
- 1 tbsp of sesame oil
- 1 tbsp of rice vinegar
- 1 tsp of sugar
- Salt and pepper to taste

Instructions:

1. Rinse the Wood Ear mushrooms under running water and pat them dry with paper towels. Cut them into thin strips and set them aside.
2. In a mixing bowl, combine the scallions, garlic, soy sauce, sesame oil, rice vinegar, sugar, salt, and pepper. Mix everything together until the sugar is dissolved.
3. Add the Wood Ear mushrooms to the mixing bowl and toss them together with the dressing until they are well-coated.
4. Allow the salad to marinate for at least 10 minutes in the refrigerator before serving.
5. Serve chilled and enjoy your delicious Wood Ear salad!

Note: You can also add other vegetables or proteins to this salad, such as cucumber, carrot, or shredded chicken, to make it a more substantial dish.

Bladderwrack Salad

Serves 4 people

Prep time: 20 minutes

Ingredients:

- 2 cups fresh Bladderwrack seaweed, chopped
- 1/4 cup red onion, chopped
- 1/4 cup fresh parsley, chopped
- 1/4 cup fresh lemon juice
- 2 tbsp olive oil
- Salt and pepper to taste

Instructions:

1. Rinse the Bladderwrack seaweed in cold water and chop it into small pieces.
2. Mix the chopped Bladderwrack, red onion, and parsley in a large bowl.
3. In a separate bowl, whisk together the lemon juice and olive oil. Add salt and pepper to taste.
4. Pour the lemon juice and olive oil mixture over the Bladderwrack salad and toss to combine.
5. Serve immediately, or refrigerate until ready to serve.

This Bladderwrack salad is a healthy and refreshing way to enjoy this nutrient-rich seaweed. It's a great addition to any meal and is perfect for those looking to incorporate more plant-based foods into their diet.

Irish Moss Pudding

Serves 4

Prep time: about 2 hours

Ingredients:

- 1/2 cup Irish moss
- 4 cups water
- 1/2 cup maple syrup
- 1/2 teaspoon vanilla extract
- 1/2 teaspoon cinnamon
- 1/4 teaspoon sea salt
- 1/4 cup almond milk
- Optional toppings: fresh fruit, chopped nuts, coconut flakes

Instructions:

1. Rinse the Irish moss in cold water to remove any dirt or debris.
2. Soak the Irish moss in water for 15-20 minutes.
3. Drain the water and rinse the Irish moss again.
4. In a large pot, add the Irish moss and 4 cups of water. Bring to a boil, then reduce heat and let simmer for about 1 hour, or until the Irish moss is tender.
5. Remove the pot from heat and let it cool for about 10 minutes.
6. Add the maple syrup, vanilla extract, cinnamon, and sea salt to the pot and stir until everything is well combined.
7. Using a blender, blend the mixture until it is smooth and creamy.
8. Pour the mixture into a bowl and let it cool to room temperature.
9. Once the mixture has cooled, add the almond milk and stir until it is well combined.
10. Place the bowl in the refrigerator and let it set for about 30 minutes to an hour, or until it reaches the desired consistency.
11. Serve the Irish moss pudding with your desired toppings.

Enjoy your delicious and healthy Irish moss pudding!

Sea Belt Salad

Servings: 4

Prep Time: 10 minutes

Ingredients:

- 1/2 pound fresh sea belt
- 2 tablespoons rice vinegar
- 1 tablespoon sesame oil
- 1 tablespoon honey
- 1 tablespoon soy sauce
- 1/2 teaspoon red pepper flakes
- 1/2 teaspoon salt
- 1/4 teaspoon black pepper
- 1/2 cup sliced cucumber
- 1/4 cup chopped scallions
- 1 tablespoon toasted sesame seeds

Directions:

1. Rinse the fresh sea belt under cold running water and pat dry with paper towels.
2. Bring a large pot of salted water to a boil. Add the sea belt and cook for 3-4 minutes or until tender.
3. Drain the sea belt and rinse with cold water. Drain again and pat dry with paper towels.
4. In a small bowl, whisk together the rice vinegar, sesame oil, honey, soy sauce, red pepper flakes, salt, and black pepper.
5. In a large bowl, combine the sea belt, sliced cucumber, and chopped scallions.
6. Pour the dressing over the sea belt mixture and toss to coat.
7. Transfer the sea belt salad to a serving platter and sprinkle with toasted sesame seeds.

Serve immediately or chill in the refrigerator until ready to serve. Enjoy!

AFTERWORD

As I reflect on the journey of researching and writing this book on wild edible plants of the Pacific Northwest, I am struck by the immense diversity and richness of this region's natural bounty. From the rugged coastline to the soaring mountains, the Pacific Northwest is home to an incredible array of edible plants that have sustained human communities for thousands of years.

It has been a privilege to delve into the history, folklore, and traditional uses of these plants and learn about their nutritional and medicinal properties. I hope this book has helped deepen your appreciation of the wild edible plants of the Pacific Northwest and perhaps inspired you to explore these foods for yourself.

Of course, as with any foraging activity, it is important to approach wild edible plants with caution and respect. It is crucial to correctly identify the plants you are harvesting, to gather them from safe and sustainable locations, and to avoid over-harvesting. It is also essential to be aware of any potential allergens or toxins that may be present in certain plants.

As you embark on your own foraging adventures, I encourage you to seek out knowledgeable guides and resources to help you navigate the rich and complex world of wild edible plants. Take the time to develop your skills and knowledge, and always approach these plants with a sense of wonder and gratitude for the abundance they provide.

Finally, I want to acknowledge the many Indigenous communities whose deep knowledge and relationship with the land have been instrumental in shaping our understanding of wild edible plants in the Pacific Northwest. I hope this book can serve as a small tribute to their wisdom and resilience and a reminder of the ongoing need to honor and respect Indigenous knowledge and sovereignty.

Thank you for joining me on this journey, and happy foraging!

ABOUT THE AUTHOR

Shannon Warner is a long-time forager and survivalist with a deep love for the outdoors. She has spent countless hours exploring the wilderness, learning about the plants and animals that inhabit it, and honing her skills in sustainable harvesting and ethical foraging. She has embarked on many adventures with her two loyal dogs by her side, from hiking and camping to hunting and fishing.

One of her core beliefs is in sustainable harvesting and ethical foraging. She firmly believes that it is possible to enjoy the bounty of nature without causing harm to the environment or depleting its resources. In her books, she provides practical tips and advice on how to forage in a way that is both sustainable and respectful of the natural world.

Whether you are an experienced forager or a beginner looking to learn more about the plants that grow in your backyard, Shannon's book is an invaluable resource that will inspire and inform you. With her expert guidance, you, too, can discover the many benefits of wild edible plants and unlock the secrets of the natural world.

Dear readers,

We hope you've enjoyed "Wild Edible Plants of the Pacific Northwest," exploring the diverse and delicious bounty nature offers. We would love to hear your thoughts on the book and how it has helped you in your foraging journey.

If you've found the book to be informative, engaging, and helpful, please consider leaving a review on Amazon. Your feedback can help others discover the joys and benefits of foraging and can also help us improve future editions.

Don't forget to share your favorite recipes and hotspots with your local foraging groups, and tag us on social media with #WildEdiblePlantsPNW. Happy foraging!

PART ELEVEN
APPENDIX

THE UNIVERSAL EDIBILTY TEST

If you are in an unfamiliar area or a survival situation, you may be unable to identify edible plants. In this case, you'd want to use the universal edibility test. As the name suggests, this test will help determine whether a plant is edible. It should only be used as a last resort, as you should ideally never be in a situation where you can't find an identifiable plant or mushroom. Always check the edibility of your harvest, even if you're sure it's safe to eat. This is important when foraging and Identify an edible plant you've never tried before.

Everyone will come across this scenario at some point. Even if you're confident that you've identified an edible plant, only try a small amount first. Even something safe to eat can make you feel unwell if you have issues with your digestion. Sometimes a food you haven't tried before doesn't agree with you, and you don't want to discover this after having a large portion. It's also possible to have an undiagnosed food allergy. Suppose you eat a lot of plant food on an empty stomach. In that case, you can quickly end up with cramps, nausea, diarrhea, or other gastrointestinal issues. An upset stomach is a quick way to ruin an otherwise enjoyable foraging trip.

Step 1: Fast for eight hours. You likely haven't eaten for at least eight hours in a survival situation like this. Still, it's essential to start on an empty stomach so that you know whether or not the plant you are testing is what has made you unwell. You can and should drink plenty of clean water, if possible.

Step 2: Check for common poisonous traits. Most toxic plants have distinguishing characteristics that are unlikely to be found on edible plants.

These include shiny, waxy leaves, spines, fine hairs, milky sap, umbrella-shaped flowers, and green or white berries. If it looks like dill or parsley, avoid it, and steer clear of anything that smells like almonds. Not every plant with these characteristics is toxic, edible dandelions have milky sap, for example, but it's an excellent rule of thumb. Rule out anything with those traits.

Step 3: Once you find a plant without any of those traits, ensure you can find plenty of specimens. Remember, the edibility test takes time, so there's not much point in going through the whole process if you can't find any more plants of that type. When you find a likely plant, break it down into separate sections, flower, leaf, stem, etc. Not every plant part is edible, even if one part is. For example, potato tubers are edible, but the plant's stem is toxic. You will need to test every aspect of the plant individually.

Step 4: Now, it's time to start testing. Select a plant part and rub it on your skin. Most people rub it on their inner forearm, the inside of their elbow, or their outer lip. Wait for fifteen minutes. If you don't experience tingling, burning, or other adverse reactions, continue with the test. If any of the above persist, you will want to choose a different plant part.

Step 5: If all is well from the step above, do a taste test with the same plant part. Put it in your mouth and don't chew or swallow; just leave it for five minutes. Spit it out and wash your mouth if you have any adverse reactions. Do the same if you taste bitterness, soapy flavors, or experience numbness. If nothing happens, continue with the test.

Step 6: Do a more extensive taste test. Now put the plant part in your mouth and chew for five minutes. Wait for any of the adverse effects mentioned above and spit out excess saliva (don't swallow anything yet). If everything seems okay after five minutes, swallow the plant part. Now the waiting begins. You need to fast for another eight hours before the next step.

Step 7: If you haven't experienced any digestive issues, you can prepare and eat one tablespoon of the plant part. If possible, it's usually safer to cook the plant part. If there are no poisoning symptoms after another eight hours of waiting, you can be sure that this plant part is edible as you prepared. It would be best if you still didn't gorge yourself, but at least you have a relatively dependable food source. You'll reduce the chance of accidental poisoning by sticking with small amounts and waiting eight hours between tasting and eating. Suppose you have significant gastrointestinal symptoms in a survival situation, like vomiting or diarrhea. In that case, you may not be able to seek medical attention.

GLOSSARY

Plant Families

Actinidiaceae - This flowering plant family has three genera and about 355 species. They consist of shrubs, small trees, and lianas. They are primarily tropical and are particularly common in Southeast Asia.

Anacardiaceae - The cashew or sumac family of flowering plants includes 83 genera and 860 species. Several species bear drupes and sometimes produce *urushiol*, which can cause skin irritation.

Apiaceae - Known as the celery, carrot, and parsley family, or umbellifers, primarily aromatic flowering plants are named after the genus Apium.

Araliaceae - There are approximately 43 genera and about 1500 species of flowering plants in this family, most of these plants are woody, and some are herbaceous.

Asparagaceae - the asparagus family of flowering plants based on the edible garden asparagus, *Asparagus officinalis*.

Aspleniaceae - The spleenwort family is a family of ferns

Asteraceae - The Compositae family was first described in the year 1740. They are called daisies, sunflowers, asters, composites, or sunflowers. With more than 32,000 species and 1,900 genera, it is the world's largest flowering plant group, rivaled only by the Orchidaceae family.

Berberidaceae - Generally known as the Barberry family, this group of flowering plants contains 18 genera.

Brassicaceae - These medium-sized flowering plants are economically important. They are commonly known as the mustards, crucifers, or cabbage family.

Caryophyllaceae - The carnation family is a family of flowering plants with about 2,625 known species.

Elaeagnaceae - The Oleaster family comprises small trees and shrubs.

Ericaceae - The heath or heather family consists of flowering plants that flourish in acidic and infertile environments. Cranberries, blueberries, huckleberries, rhododendron (including azaleas), and a wide range of heaths and heathers are examples of well-known members.

Euphorbiaceae - Among flowering plants, the spurge family is one of the largest. They are also commonly known as euphorbias in English, their genus name. Most spurges are herbs, such as Euphorbia paralias, but some are shrubs or trees, particularly in the tropics.

Lamiaceae [LAY-mee-AY-see-ee] The mint or deadnettle family is aromatic in all parts. They include widely used culinary herbs like basil, mint, rosemary, sage, savory, marjoram, oregano, hyssop, thyme, lavender, and perilla. Catnip, salvia, bee balm, wild dagga, and oriental motherwort are medicinal herbs.

Malvaceae - The Mallow family of flowering plants is estimated to contain 244 genera with 4225 known species. Among the well-known members of this plant family are okra, cotton, cacao, and durian.

Menispermaceae - The moonseed family comprises 440 species, most of which are found in low-lying tropical regions, with some species also found in temperate and arid regions.

Morchellaceae -

Oxalidaceae - The wood sorrel family comprises five genera of herbaceous plants, shrubs, and small trees, with about 570 species in the Oxalis genus.

Plantaginaceae - The Plantain family and order Lamiales include common flower species such as snapdragon and foxglove.

Polygonaceae - The knotweed or smartweed-buckwheat family is an informal name for a family of flowering plants. There are about 1200 species within about 48 genera. There are members of this family worldwide, but they are most abundant in the North Temperate Zone.

Portulacaceae - The purslane family is a family of flowering plants with 115 species in one genus, Portulaca.

Ranunculaceae - the buttercup or crowfoot family is a family of over 2,000 known flowering plants in 43 genera distributed worldwide.

Rosaceae - The rose family includes 4,828 species of flowering plants.

Tremellaceae -

Viburnaceae - was previously known as the Adoxaceae family and is commonly known as the Moschatel family. About 150–200 species belong to this family of flowering plants.

Plant Types

Annual [AN-YOO-*UHL*] - Plants without a permanent woody stem. They are usually flowering garden plants or potherbs.

Deciduous [DIH-SIJ-OO-UHS] - After the growing season, the plant sheds leaves and turns dormant.

Dioecious [DAHY-EE-SH*UH*S] - having the male and female organs in separate and distinct individuals, having different sexes.

Herbaceous [HUR-BEY-SH*UH*S] - low-growing plants with soft green stems. Their above-ground growth is often seasonal.

Monoecious [MUH-NEE-SHUHS] - having the stamens and the pistils in separate flowers on the same plant.

Perennial [PUH-REN-EE-UHL] - It usually lasts for more than two years. These plants don't have a lot of woody growth.

Plant Parts

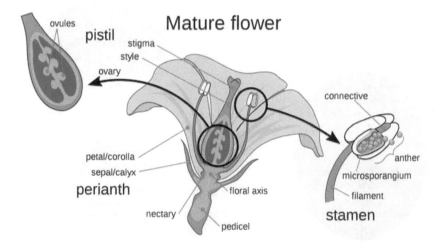

Achene [*UH*-KEEN] - a small, dry one-seeded fruit that does not open to release the seed.

Anther [AN-THER] - the pollen-bearing part of a stamen.

Filament [FIL-*uh*-MU*h*NT] - the stalklike portion of a stamen, supporting the anther.
Ligulate [LIG-YU*h*-LIT] - strap-shaped, such as the ray florets of daisy family plants.
Peltate [PEL-TEYT] - fixed to the stalk by the center or by some point distinctly within the margin.
Petiole [PET-EE-OHL] - the slender stalk by which a leaf is attached to the stem; leafstalk.
Pistil [PIS-TL] - the ovule-bearing or seed-bearing female organ of a flower, consisting when complete of the ovary, style, and stigma.
Pith [PITH] - The soft central cylinder of tissue in the plant's stem.
Sepal [SEE-PU*h*L] - The outer parts of the flower (often green and leaf-like) that enclose a developing bud.
Sessile [SES-IL] - attached directly by its base without a stalk or peduncle.
Stamen [STEY-MU*h*N] - the pollen-bearing organ of a flower, consisting of the filament and the anther.
Staminodia [STAM-*uh*-NOH-DEE-*uh*] - A stamen that is sterile or abortive.
Whorled [WURL'D] - The arrangement of like parts around a point on an axis, such as leaves or flowers;

Leaf Types

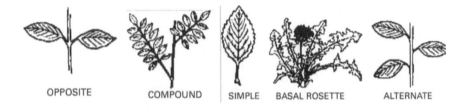

OPPOSITE   COMPOUND   SIMPLE   BASAL ROSETTE   ALTERNATE

Alternate - The leaves are single at each node and spiral upwards along the stem.
Basal leaf - a leaf that grows lowest on the stem of a plant or flower.
Compound -
Opposite -
Palmate [PAL-MEYT] - Having four or more lobes or leaflets.
Palmately compound - A petiole's tip is attached to a leaflet.
Pinnate [PIN-EYT] - Each side of a stalk is divided into leaflets
Rosette [ROH-ZET] - a circular arrangement of leaves or structures resembling leaves.
Simple - Leaves with a single, undivided lamina
Tripinnately compound - Leaf made up of three pinnate parts.

Leaf Shapes

LANCE-SHAPED ELLIPTIC EGG-SHAPED OBLONG WEDGE-SHAPED TRIANGULAR LONG-POINTED TOP-SHAPED

Cordate [KAWR-DEYT] - heart-shaped.

217

Elliptical [IH-LIP-TI-KUHL] - Planar, shaped like a flattened circle, symmetrical about the long and short axes, tapering equally to the tip and the base; oval.
Lanceolate [AN-SEE-UH-LEYT] - shaped like the head of a lance, having a rounded base and a tapering apex.
Long-pointed - Lying close and flat and pointing toward the plant's apex or structure.
Oblanceolate [OB-LAN-SEE-UH-LIT] - having a rounded apex and a tapering base.
Oblong [OB-LAWNG]- Having a length a few times greater than the width, with sides almost parallel and ends rounded.
Ovate [OH-VEYT] - egg-shaped, having such a shape with a broader end at the base.
Triangular [TRAHY-ANG-GYUH-LER] - Planar with three sides.
Wedge - narrowly triangular, wider at the apex, and tapering toward the base.

Flower Types

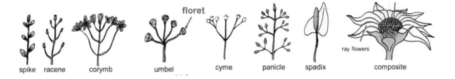

Corymb [KAWR-IMB] - a form of inflorescence in which the flowers form a flat-topped or convex cluster, the outermost flowers being the first to open.
Composite [KUHM-POZ-IT] is characterized by alternate, opposite, or *whorled* leaves and a whorl of bracts surrounding its flower heads. These flower heads typically extend from a disk containing tiny petal-less flowers and from the disk's rim to a ray of petals.
Cyme [SAHYM] - an inflorescence in which the primary axis bears a single central or terminal flower that blooms first.
Inflorescence [IN-FLAW-RES-UHNS] - the complete flower head of a plant, including stems, stalks, bracts, and flowers.
Panicle [PAN-I-KUHL] - any loose, diversely branching flower cluster.
Raceme [REY-SEEM] - a flower cluster with separate flowers attached by short equal stalks at equal distances along a central stem. The flowers at the base of the main stem develop first.
Spike [SPAHYK] - a type of racemose inflorescence.
Spadix [SPEY-DIKS] - an inflorescence consisting of a spike with a fleshy or thickened axis, usually enclosed in a spathe.
Umbel or Subumbel [UHM-BUHL] - consisting of several short flower stalks that spread from a common point, like umbrella ribs.

Fruit/Berry

Aggregate fruit [AG-RI-GIT FROOT]- composed of a cluster of carpels belonging to the same flower as the raspberry.
Dehiscent [DI ! HI SƏNT] - opens to release seeds or pollen
Drupe [DROOP] - a fleshy fruit with thin skin and a central stone containing the seed, e.g., a plum, cherry, almond, or olive.
Elaiosome [EH-LAY-UH-SOHM] - an oil-rich body on seeds or fruits that attract ants and act as dispersal agents.
Globoid [GLOH-BOID] - approximately globular. Globe-shaped; spherical.
Infructescence [IN-FRUC-TES-CENCE] - an aggregate fruit.

Myrmecochory [MIR-MI-KAW-KUH-REE] - the dispersal of fruits and seeds by ants.
Syconium [SAHY-KOH-NEE-UHM] - a fleshy hollow receptacle that develops into a multifruit.

Bark & Roots

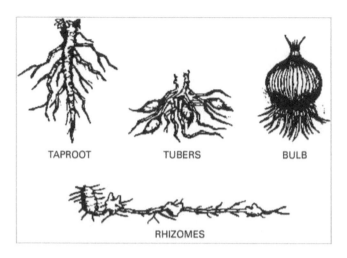

TAPROOT   TUBERS   BULB

RHIZOMES

Acaulescent [AK-AW-LES-UHNT] - stemless
Lenticel [LEN-TUH-SEL] - One of the many holes in a woody plant's stem that allows air to exchange between the inside and outside.

Medical Terms

Amygdalin [UH-MIG-DUH-LIN] - White, bitter-tasting glycosidic powder usually obtained from the leaves and seeds of plants of the genus Prunus and related genera: used mainly as an expectorant in medicine.
Anthocyanins [AN-THUH-SAHY-UH-NIN] - These flavonoids are known for their pigmentation properties, responsible for fruits, vegetables, flowers, and cereals' red, purple, and blue colors.
Astringent [UH-STRIN-JUHNT] - Contracting the body's tissues or canals reduces mucus or blood discharges.
Berberine [BUR-BUH-REEN] - Known as an antipyretic, antibacterial, and stomachic, this crystalline, water-soluble alkaloid is derived from barberry or goldenseal.
Carotenoid [KUH-ROT-N-OID] - Red or yellow pigments, similar to carotene, found in animal fat and some plants.
Cyanogenic glycosides - chemical compounds contained in foods that release hydrogen cyanide when chewed or digested.
Demulcent [DIH-MUHL-SUHNT] - a substance that relieves irritation of the mucous membranes in the mouth by forming a protective film.
Depurative [DEP-YUH-REY-TIV] - herbs considered to have purifying and detoxifying effects.
Flavonoids [FLEY-VUH-NOID] - An antioxidant, antiviral, anticancer, anti-inflammatory, and anti-allergenic group of water-soluble polyphenols found in plants.
Hydrocyanic acid - scientific word for cyanide.
Lycopene [LAHY-KUH-PEEN] - Red crystalline substance found in some fruits, including tomatoes and paprika.

Odontalgic [OH-DON-TAL-JUH] - toothache.

Prunasin [PRŪ-Nə-SəN] - A cyanogenic glucoside related to amygdalin found in Prunus species.

Urolithiasis [YOOR-OH-LI-THAHY-UH-SIS] - A disease where stones form in the urinary tract.

Urushiol [OO-ROO-SHEE-AWL] - The active irritant principle in several plant species in the Rhus genus.

General definitions

Anthropogenic [AN-THRUH-PUH-JEN-IK] - caused by humans.

Glaucous [GLAW-KUHS] - covered with a whitish bloom, as a plum.

Siliceous [SUH-LISH-UHS] - growing in soil rich in silica.

Calcareous [KAL-KAIR-EE-UHS] - occurring on chalk or limestone.

Monoecious [MUH-NEE-SHUHS] - THE STAMENS AND PISTILS ARE IN SEPARATE FLOWERS ON THE SAME PLANT.

Mucilaginous [MYOO-SUH-LAJ-UH-NUHS] - having a viscous or gelatinous consistency.

PHOTO ATTRIBUTIONS

Rubus allegheniensis Porter observed in the United States of America by Sandy Wolkenberg (licensed under http://creativecommons.org/licenses/by/4.0/)

Rubus allegheniensis Porter observed in the United States of America by Andrew Garn (licensed under http://creativecommons.org/licenses/by/4.0/)

Sambucus canadensis L. observed in the United States of America by Kim (licensed under http://creativecommons.org/licenses/by/4.0/)

Sambucus canadensis L. observed in the United States of America by mfeaver (licensed under http://creativecommons.org/licenses/by/4.0/)

Rosa canina L. observed in the United States of America by Chris Johnson (licensed under http://creativecommons.org/licenses/by/4.0/)

Stellaria media (L.) Vill. observed in the United States of America by giantcicada (licensed under http://creativecommons.org/licenses/by/4.0/)

Stellaria media (L.) Vill. observed in the United States of America by Randy A Nonenmacher (licensed under http://creativecommons.org/licenses/by/4.0/)

BIBLIOGRAPHY

Abies lasiocarpa | Landscape Plants | Oregon State University. (n.d.-a). https://landscapeplants.oregonstate.edu/plants/abies-lasiocarpa

Abies lasiocarpa | Landscape Plants | Oregon State University. (n.d.-b). https://landscapeplants.oregonstate.edu/plants/abies-lasiocarpa

Abies lasiocarpa Subalpine Fir, Alpine Fir PFAF Plant Database. (n.d.). https://pfaf.org/User/Plant.aspx?LatinName=Abies+lasiocarpa

Achillea millefolium. (n.d.). https://www.wnps.org/native-plant-directory/6/achillea-millefolium

Achillea millefolium - Plant Finder. (n.d.). https://www.missouribotanicalgarden.org/PlantFinder/PlantFinderDetails.aspx?kempercode=b282

Achillea millefolium (Common Yarrow, Devil's Nettle, Dog Daisy, Dog Fennel, Milfoil, Soldier's Woundwort, Thousandleaf, Westen Yarrow, Yarrow) | North Carolina Extension Gardener Plant Toolbox. (n.d.). https://plants.ces.ncsu.edu/plants/achillea-millefolium/

Achillea millefolium Yarrow, Boreal yarrow, California yarrow, Giant yarrow, Coast yarrow, Western yarrow, Pacific yarrow PFAF Plant Database. (n.d.). https://pfaf.org/user/plant.aspx?LatinName=Achillea+millefolium

Agarum clathratum Dumortier :: AlgaeBase. (n.d.). https://www.algaebase.org/search/species/detail/?species_id=19602

Aisa, H. A., Xin, X., & Tang, D. (2020). Chemical constituents and their pharmacological activities of plants from Cichorium genus. *Chinese Herbal Medicines, 12*(3), 224–236. https://doi.org/10.1016/j.chmed.2020.05.001

Alaria marginata Postels & Ruprecht :: AlgaeBase. (n.d.). https://www.algaebase.org/search/species/detail/?species_id=3649

Alfalfa Herbal Medicine, Health Benefits, Side Effects. (n.d.). http://www.medicalhealthguide.com/herb/alfalfa.htm

Anaphalis margaritacea (Pearly Everlasting, Sweet Everlasting, Western Pearly Everlasting) | North Carolina Extension Gardener Plant Toolbox. (n.d.). https://plants.ces.ncsu.edu/plants/anaphalis-margaritacea/

Anaphalis margaritacea - Plant Finder. (n.d.). https://www.missouribotanicalgarden.org/PlantFinder/PlantFinderDetails.aspx?taxonid=277132&isprofile=0&

Anaphalis margaritacea (Pearly Everlasting): Minnesota Wildflowers. (n.d.). https://www.minnesotawildflowers.info/flower/pearly-everlasting

Anaphalis margaritacea Pearly Everlasting, Western pearly everlasting PFAF Plant Database. (n.d.). https://pfaf.org/user/Plant.aspx?LatinName=Anaphalis+margaritacea

Arbutus menziesii | Landscape Plants | Oregon State University. (n.d.). https://landscapeplants.oregonstate.edu/plants/arbutus-menziesii

Arbutus menziesii (Madrona, Madrone, Pacific Madrone) | North Carolina Extension Gardener Plant Toolbox. (n.d.). https://plants.ces.ncsu.edu/plants/arbutus-menziesii/

Arbutus menziesii Madrona, Pacific madrone, Pacific Madrone PFAF Plant Database. (n.d.). https://pfaf.org/user/Plant.aspx?LatinName=Arbutus+menziesii

Bales, A. L., & Hersch-Green, E. I. (2019). Effects of soil nitrogen on diploid advantage in fireweed, Chamerion angustifolium (Onagraceae). *Ecology and Evolution, 9*(3), 1095–1109. https://doi.org/10.1002/ece3.4797

Beach pea • Lathyrus japonicus. (n.d.). Biodiversity of the Central Coast. https://www.centralcoastbiodiversity.org/beach-pea-bull-lathyrus-japonicus.html

Bennett, J. (2023, March 19). *Can Dogs Safely Eat Indian Plum? - What Dog Owners Need to Know.* Winnipups. https://winnipups.com/can-dogs-eat-indian-plum/

Betula papyrifera | Landscape Plants | Oregon State University. (n.d.). https://landscapeplants.oregonstate.edu/plants/betula-papyrifera

Betula papyrifera (Canoe Birch, Kenai Birch, Mountain Paper Birch, Paperbark birch, Paper Birch, White Birch) | North Carolina Extension Gardener Plant Toolbox. (n.d.). https://plants.ces.ncsu.edu/plants/betula-papyrifera/

Betula papyrifera (paper birch): Go Botany. (n.d.). https://gobotany.nativeplanttrust.org/species/betula/papyrifera/

Betula papyrifera Paper Birch, Mountain paper birch, Kenai birch PFAF Plant Database. (n.d.). https://pfaf.org/User/Plant.aspx?LatinName=Betula+papyrifera

Bitter Cherry - Prunus emarginata - PNW Plants. (n.d.). Copyright (C) 2006 Filaret Ilas. All Rights Reserved. http://pnwplants.wsu.edu/PlantDisplay.aspx?PlantID=294

Black Cottonwood - Populus trichocarpa - PNW Plants. (n.d.). Copyright (C) 2006 Filaret Ilas. All Rights Reserved. http://www.pnwplants.wsu.edu/PlantDisplay.aspx?PlantID=217

Candy Cap - Bay Area Mycological Society. (n.d.). Text and Images Copyright Bay Area Mycological Society and the Authors Except Where Noted. All Rights Reserved. http://bayareamushrooms.org/mushroommonth/candy_cap.html

Caulerpa lentillifera, Small seagrape : fisheries, aquaculture. (n.d.). https://www.sealifebase.se/summary/Caulerpa-lentillifera.html

Caulerpa lentillifera J.Agardh :: AlgaeBase. (n.d.). https://www.algaebase.org/search/species/detail/?species_id=3754

Chamerion angustifolium - Plant Finder. (n.d.). https://www.missouribotanicalgarden.org/PlantFinder/PlantFinderDetails.aspx?taxonid=297622

Chandrasekara, A., & Shahidi, F. (2018). Herbal beverages: Bioactive compounds and their role in disease risk reduction - A review. *Journal of Traditional and Complementary Medicine*, 8(4), 451–458. https://doi.org/10.1016/j.jtcme.2017.08.006

Chickweed Herbal Medicine, Health Benefits, Side Effects. (n.d.). http://www.medicalhealthguide.com/herb/chickweed.htm

Chlorophyllum rachodes | Urban Mushrooms. (n.d.). https://urbanmushrooms.com/index.php?id=5

Chlorophyllum rhacodes: The Ultimate Mushroom Guide. (n.d.). Mushroom Identification - Ultimate Mushroom Library. https://ultimate-mushroom.com/edible/50-chlorophyllum-rhacodes.html

Cho, M., Lee, D., Kim, J., & You, S. (2014). Molecular characterization and immunomodulatory activity of sulfated fucans from Agarum cribrosum. *Carbohydrate Polymers*, 113, 507–514. https://doi.org/10.1016/j.carbpol.2014.07.055

Chondrus crispus Stackhouse. (n.d.). https://www.seaweed.ie/descriptions/Chondrus_crispus.php

Cichorium intybus (Blue Sailors, Chicory, Coffeeweed, Common Chicory, Cornflower, Italian Dandelion, Succory) | North Carolina Extension Gardener Plant Toolbox. (n.d.). https://plants.ces.ncsu.edu/plants/cichorium-intybus/

Cichorium intybus Chicory, Radicchio, Succory, Witloof PFAF Plant Database. (n.d.). https://pfaf.org/user/plant.aspx?LatinName=Cichorium+intybus

Comb Tooth Fungus Identification: Pictures, Habitat, Season & Spore Print | Hericium coralloides. (n.d.). https://www.ediblewildfood.com/comb-tooth-fungus.aspx

Corylus Cornuta Beaked Hazel, California hazelnut, Turkish Filbert, Turkish Hazel PFAF Plant Database. (n.d.). https://pfaf.org/user/Plant.aspx?LatinName=Corylus+Cornuta

Corylus cornuta (Beaked Hazelnut) | North Carolina Extension Gardener Plant Toolbox. (n.d.). https://plants.ces.ncsu.edu/plants/corylus-cornuta/

Corylus cornuta: Beaked Hazelnut | Portland Nursery. (n.d.). https://www.portlandnursery.com/natives/corylus

Crataegus douglasii (Aubepine, Black Haw, Black Hawthorn, Blackthorn, Douglass Hawthorn, Haw Apple, Hawthorn, May Bush, Oxyacantha, Pirliteiro, Red Hawthorn, Thorn Apple, Thorn Plum, Weisdornbluten) | North Carolina Extension Gardener Plant Toolbox. (n.d.). https://plants.ces.ncsu.edu/plants/crataegus-douglasii/

Crataegus douglasii Black Hawthorn PFAF Plant Database. (n.d.). https://pfaf.org/user/plant.aspx?LatinName=Crataegus+douglasii

D. (2017a, September 9). *Hawthorn Harvest - Eat The Weeds and other things, too.* Eat the Weeds and Other Things, Too. https://www.eattheweeds.com/the-crataegus-clan-food-poison-2/

D. (2019, December 1). *Chickweed Chic - Eat The Weeds and other things, too.* Eat the Weeds and Other Things, Too. https://www.eattheweeds.com/chickweed-connoisseurs-2/

Dandelion. (n.d.). Mount Sinai Health System. https://www.mountsinai.org/health-library/herb/dandelion

Daneshfar, A., Hashemi, P., Delfan, B., Tavakkoli, M., & Rashno, P. M. (2017). The Efficient Extraction of Phenolic Compounds from Oak Gall Using a Miniaturized Matrix Solid-Phase Dispersion Method before their HPLC Determination. *Herbal Medicines Journal, 2*(2), 71–79. https://doi.org/10.22087/hmj.v0i0.615

Domínguez, H., & Loret, E. (2019). Ulva lactuca, A Source of Troubles and Potential Riches. *Marine Drugs, 17*(6), 357. https://doi.org/10.3390/md17060357

Du Preez, R., Majzoub, M. E., Thomas, T., Panchal, S. K., & Brown, L. (2020). Caulerpa lentillifera (Sea Grapes) Improves Cardiovascular and Metabolic Health of Rats with Diet-Induced Metabolic Syndrome. *Metabolites, 10*(12), 500. https://doi.org/10.3390/metabo10120500

E-Flora BC Atlas Page. (n.d.). http://linnet.geog.ubc.ca/Atlas/Atlas.aspx?sciname=Clinopodium%20douglasii

Egregia | MARINe. (n.d.). https://marine.ucsc.edu/target/target-species-egregia.html

Egregia menziesii (Turner) Areschoug :: AlgaeBase. (n.d.). https://www.algaebase.org/search/species/detail/?species_id=4872

Epilobium angustifolium (Almaruat, Blooming Sally, Bomb Weed, Fireweed, Fire Weed, French willow, Great Willowherb, Great Willow Herb, Rose bay, Rosebay Willowherb, Saint Anthony's Laurel, Willow Herb) | North Carolina Extension Gardener Plant Toolbox. (n.d.). https://plants.ces.ncsu.edu/plants/epilobium-angustifolium/

Equisetum arvense (Common Horsetail, Field Horsetail, Horsetail, Scouring rush, Western horsetail) | North Carolina Extension Gardener Plant Toolbox. (n.d.). https://plants.ces.ncsu.edu/plants/equisetum-arvense/

Equisetum arvense (Field Horsetail): Minnesota Wildflowers. (n.d.). https://www.minnesotawildflowers.info/fern/field-horsetail

equisetum arvense Field Horsetail PFAF Plant Database. (n.d.). https://pfaf.org/user/Plant.aspx?LatinName=equisetum+arvense

FeralFungi. (n.d.). *Oregon Reishi (Ganoderma oregonense).* https://feralfungi.com/products/oregon-reishi-extract?variant=39491536879773

Fireweed (Chamerion angustifolium). (n.d.). https://www.illinoiswildflowers.info/prairie/plantx/fireweedx.htm

Food as MedicinePurslane (Portulaca oleracea, Portulacaceae) - American Botanical Council. (n.d.). https://www.herbalgram.org/resources/herbalegram/volumes/volume-18/issue-8-august-2021/news-and-features/food-as-medicine-purslane/

Fucus vesiculosus Linnaeus :: AlgaeBase. (n.d.). https://www.algaebase.org/search/species/detail/?species_id=87

Gaultheria shallon | Landscape Plants | Oregon State University. (n.d.). https://landscapeplants.oregonstate.edu/plants/gaultheria-shallon

Gaultheria shallon (Oregon Wintergreen, Salal, Shallon) | North Carolina Extension Gardener Plant Toolbox. (n.d.). https://plants.ces.ncsu.edu/plants/gaultheria-shallon/

Gaultheria shallon Shallon, Salal PFAF Plant Database. (n.d.). https://pfaf.org/User/plant.aspx?latinname=Gaultheria+shallon

Glycyrrhiza lepidota American Liquorice PFAF Plant Database. (n.d.). https://pfaf.org/user/Plant.aspx?LatinName=Glycyrrhiza+lepidota

Glycyrrhiza lepidota (Wild Licorice): Minnesota Wildflowers. (n.d.). https://www.minnesotawildflowers.info/flower/wild-licorice

Gründemann, C., Lengen, K., Sauer, B., Garcia-Käufer, M., Zehl, M., & Huber, R. (2014). Equisetum arvense (common horsetail) modulates the function of inflammatory immunocompetent cells. *BMC Complementary and Alternative Medicine, 14*(1). https://doi.org/10.1186/1472-6882-14-283

H. (2014a, February 10). *Sitka Spruce, Picea sitchensis*. Native Plants PNW. http://nativeplantspnw.com/sitka-spruce-picea-sitchensis/

H. (2014b, March 19). *Subalpine Fir, Abies lasiocarpa*. Native Plants PNW. http://nativeplantspnw.com/subalpine-fir-abies-lasiocarpa/

H. (2014c, April 9). *Shore Pine, Pinus contorta*. Native Plants PNW. http://nativeplantspnw.com/shore-pine-pinus-contorta/

H. (2014d, May 28). *Pacific Madrone, Arbutus menziesii*. Native Plants PNW. http://nativeplantspnw.com/pacific-madrone-arbutus-menziesii/

H. (2014e, September 15). *Oregon White Oak, Quercus garryana*. Native Plants PNW. http://nativeplantspnw.com/oregon-white-oak-quercus-garryana/

H. (2014f, November 17). *Pacific Crabapple, Malus fusca*. Native Plants PNW. http://nativeplantspnw.com/pacific-crabapple-malus-fusca/

H. (2015a, March 4). *Bitter Cherry, Prunus emarginata*. Native Plants PNW. http://nativeplantspnw.com/bitter-cherry-prunus-emarginata/

H. (2015b, March 23). *Black Hawthorns, Crataegus douglasii & C. suksdorfii*. Native Plants PNW. http://nativeplantspnw.com/black-hawthorns-crataegus-douglasii-c-suksdorfii/

H. (2015c, March 23). *Black Hawthorns, Crataegus douglasii & C. suksdorfii*. Native Plants PNW. http://nativeplantspnw.com/black-hawthorns-crataegus-douglasii-c-suksdorfii/

H. (2015d, September 28). *Salal, Gaultheria shallon*. Native Plants PNW. http://nativeplantspnw.com/salal-gaultheria-shallon/

H. (2016a, January 18). *Beaked Hazelnut, Corylus cornuta*. Native Plants PNW. http://nativeplantspnw.com/beaked-hazelnut-corylus-cornuta/

H. (2016b, February 8). *Red Huckleberry, Vaccinium parvifolium*. Native Plants PNW. http://nativeplantspnw.com/red-huckleberry-vaccinium-parvifolium/

H. (2016c, March 21). *Ocean Spray, Holodiscus discolor*. Native Plants PNW. https://nativeplantspnw.com/ocean-spray-holodiscus-discolor/

H. (2016d, April 4). *Indian Plum, Oemleria cerasiformis*. Native Plants PNW. https://nativeplantspnw.com/indian-plum-oemleria-cerasiformis/

H. (2016e, June 6). *Western Mountain Ash, Sorbus scopulina*. Native Plants PNW. https://nativeplantspnw.com/western-mountain-ash-sorbus-scopulina/

H. (2016f, June 27). *Nootka Rose, Rosa nutkana*. Native Plants PNW. https://nativeplantspnw.com/nootka-rose-rosa-nutkana/

H. (2016g, July 18). *Blackcap Raspberry, Rubus leucodermis*. Native Plants PNW. https://nativeplantspnw.com/blackcap-raspberry-rubus-leucodermis/

H. (2016h, July 25). *Thimbleberry, Rubus parviflorus*. Native Plants PNW. https://nativeplantspnw.com/thimbleberry-rubus-parviflorus/

H. (2016i, August 1). *Salmonberry, Rubus spectabilis*. Native Plants PNW. https://nativeplantspnw.com/salmonberry-rubus-spectabilis/

H. (2016j, September 26). *Coast Black Gooseberry, Ribes divaricatum*. Native Plants PNW. https://nativeplantspnw.com/coast-black-gooseberry-ribes-divaricatum/

H. (2017b, January 16). *Trumpet Honeysuckle, Lonicera ciliosa*. Native Plants PNW. http://nativeplantspnw.com/trumpet-honeysuckle-lonicera-ciliosa/

H. (2017c, March 13). *Blue Elderberry, Sambucus nigra ssp. cerulea*. Native Plants PNW. https://nativeplantspnw.com/blue-elderberry-sambucus-nigra-ssp-cerulea/

Habtemariam, S. (2020). Trametes versicolor (Synn. Coriolus versicolor) Polysaccharides in Cancer Therapy: Targets and Efficacy. *Biomedicines, 8*(5), 135. https://doi.org/10.3390/biomedicines8050135

Hayashi, H., Miwa, E., & Inoue, K. (2005). Phylogenetic Relationship of Glycyrrhiza lepidota,

American Licorice, in Genus Glycyrrhiza Based on rbcL Sequences and Chemical Constituents. *Biological & Pharmaceutical Bulletin, 28*(1), 161–164. https://doi.org/10.1248/bpb.28.161

Holodiscus discolor | Landscape Plants | Oregon State University. (n.d.). https://landscapeplants.oregonstate.edu/plants/holodiscus-discolor

Holodiscus discolor Creambush, Oceanspray PFAF Plant Database. (n.d.). https://pfaf.org/user/Plant.aspx?LatinName=Holodiscus+discolor

Hummer, K. E. (2010). Rubus Pharmacology: Antiquity to the Present. *Hortscience, 45*(11), 1587–1591. https://doi.org/10.21273/hortsci.45.11.1587

Janda, K., Gutowska, I., Geszke-Moritz, M., & Jakubczyk, K. (2021). The Common Cichory (Cichorium intybus L.) as a Source of Extracts with Health-Promoting Properties—A Review. *Molecules, 26*(6), 1814. https://doi.org/10.3390/molecules26061814

Kansas Wildflowers and Grasses - Wild licorice. (n.d.). https://www.kswildflower.org/flower_details.php?flowerID=231

Karimi, E., Ebrahimi, M., Oskoueian, A., Omidvar, V., Hendra, R., & Nazeran, H. (2013). Insight into the functional and medicinal properties of Medicago sativa (Alfalfa) leaves extract. *Journal of Medicinal Plants Research, 7*(7), 290–297. https://doi.org/10.5897/jmpr11.1663

Lady Bird Johnson Wildflower Center - The University of Texas at Austin. (n.d.). https://www.wildflower.org/plants/result.php?id_plant=maaq2

Laminaria digitata. (n.d.). https://www.seaweed.ie/descriptions/Laminaria_digitata.php

Laminaria digitata (Hudson) J.V.Lamouroux :: AlgaeBase. (n.d.). https://www.algaebase.org/search/species/detail/?species_id=165272

Lathyrus japonicus Beach Pea, Smallflower beach pea PFAF Plant Database. (n.d.). https://pfaf.org/user/Plant.aspx?LatinName=Lathyrus+japonicus

Lathyrus japonicus (Beach Pea): Minnesota Wildflowers. (n.d.). https://www.minnesotawildflowers.info/flower/beach-pea

Lathyrus japonicus (beach vetchling): Go Botany. (n.d.). https://gobotany.nativeplanttrust.org/species/lathyrus/japonicus/

Limnanthes alba - FNA. (n.d.). http://beta.floranorthamerica.org/Limnanthes_alba

Limnanthes alba Meadowfoam, White meadowfoam PFAF Plant Database. (n.d.). https://pfaf.org/user/Plant.aspx?LatinName=Limnanthes+alba

Lonicera ciliosa. (n.d.). https://www.wnps.org/native-plant-directory/152-lonicera-ciliosa

Lonicera ciliosa | Landscape Plants | Oregon State University. (n.d.). https://landscapeplants.oregonstate.edu/plants/lonicera-ciliosa

Lonicera ciliosa Orange Honeysuckle PFAF Plant Database. (n.d.). https://pfaf.org/User/Plant.aspx?LatinName=Lonicera+ciliosa

Lysichiton americanus. (n.d.). https://www.wnps.org/native-plant-directory/159-lysichiton-americanus

Lysichiton americanus Yellow Skunk Cabbage, American skunkcabbage PFAF Plant Database. (n.d.). https://pfaf.org/user/Plant.aspx?LatinName=Lysichiton+americanus

Mahboubi, M. (2021). Sambucus nigra (black elder) as alternative treatment for cold and flu. *Advances in Traditional Medicine, 21*(3), 405–414. https://doi.org/10.1007/s13596-020-00469-z

Mahonia aquifolium | Landscape Plants | Oregon State University. (n.d.). https://landscapeplants.oregonstate.edu/plants/mahonia-aquifolium

Mahonia aquifolium Oregon Grape, Hollyleaved barberry, Oregon Holly Grape, Oregon Holly PFAF Plant Database. (n.d.). https://pfaf.org/user/plant.aspx?latinname=Mahonia+aquifolium

Malus fusca | Landscape Plants | Oregon State University. (n.d.). https://landscapeplants.oregonstate.edu/plants/malus-fusca

Malus fusca Oregon Crab, Oregon crab apple PFAF Plant Database. (n.d.). https://pfaf.org/user/Plant.aspx?LatinName=Malus+fusca

MarLIN - The Marine Life Information Network - Bladder wrack (Fucus vesiculosus). (n.d.). https://www.marlin.ac.uk/species/detail/1330

Mármol, I., Sánchez-De-Diego, C., Jiménez-Moreno, N., Ancín-Azpilicueta, C., & Rodríguez-Yoldi, M. J. (2017). Therapeutic Applications of Rose Hips from Different Rosa Species. *International Journal of Molecular Sciences*, 18(6), 1137. https://doi.org/10.3390/ijms18061137

Maryland Biodiversity Project - Red Clover (Trifolium pratense). (n.d.). https://www.marylandbiodiversity.com/view/3860

Medicago sativa. (n.d.-a). https://www.fs.usda.gov/database/feis/plants/forb/medsat/all.html

Medicago sativa. (n.d.-b). https://ucjeps.berkeley.edu/eflora/eflora_display.php?tid=32943

Medicago sativa Alfalfa, Yellow alfalfa PFAF Plant Database. (n.d.). https://pfaf.org/user/plant.aspx?LatinName=Medicago+sativa

Medicago sativa Calflora. (n.d.). https://www.calflora.org/app/taxon?crn=5387

Moerman, D. E. (1998). *Native American Ethnobotany*. Timber Press (OR).

Mountain, M. (2023, February 1). *Lion's Mane "Tufted" – (Hericium americanum)*. Mushroom Mountain. https://mushroommountain.com/lions-mane-tufted-hericium-americanum/

MushroomExpert.Com. (n.d.-a). *Chlorophyllum rhacodes (MushroomExpert.Com)*. https://www.mushroomexpert.com/chlorophyllum_rhacodes.html

MushroomExpert.Com. (n.d.-b). *Craterellus tubaeformis (MushroomExpert.Com)*. https://www.mushroomexpert.com/craterellus_tubaeformis.html

MushroomExpert.Com. (n.d.-c). *Ganoderma oregonense (MushroomExpert.Com)*. https://www.mushroomexpert.com/ganoderma_oregonense.html

MushroomExpert.Com. (n.d.-d). *Hericium americanum (MushroomExpert.Com)*. https://www.mushroomexpert.com/hericium_americanum.html

MushroomExpert.Com. (n.d.-e). *Hericium coralloides (MushroomExpert.Com)*. https://www.mushroomexpert.com/hericium_coralloides.html

MushroomExpert.Com. (n.d.-f). *Lactarius deliciosus group (MushroomExpert.Com)*. https://www.mushroomexpert.com/lactarius_deliciosus.html

MushroomExpert.Com. (n.d.-g). *Lactarius rubidus (MushroomExpert.Com)*. https://www.mushroomexpert.com/lactarius_rubidus.html

MushroomExpert.Com. (n.d.-h). *Trametes versicolor: The Turkey Tail (MushroomExpert.Com)*. https://www.mushroomexpert.com/trametes_versicolor.html

Nootka Rose - Rosa nutkana - PNW Plants. (n.d.). Copyright (C) 2006 Filaret Ilas. All Rights Reserved. http://pnwplants.wsu.edu/PlantDisplay.aspx?PlantID=301

Obluchinskaya, E. D., Pozharitskaya, O. N., Zakharov, D., Flisyuk, E. V., Terninko, I. I., Generalova, Y. E., Smekhova, I. E., & Shikov, A. N. (2022). The Biochemical Composition and Antioxidant Properties of Fucus vesiculosus from the Arctic Region. *Marine Drugs*, 20(3), 193. https://doi.org/10.3390/md20030193

Oemleria cerasiformis. (n.d.). https://www.wnps.org/native-plant-directory/172-oemleria-cerasiformis

Oemleria cerasiformis | Landscape Plants | Oregon State University. (n.d.). https://landscapeplants.oregonstate.edu/plants/oemleria-cerasiformis

Oemleria cerasiformis Oso Berry, Indian plum PFAF Plant Database. (n.d.). https://pfaf.org/user/Plant.aspx?LatinName=Oemleria+cerasiformis

Oladeji, O. S., & Oyebamiji, A. K. (2020). Stellaria media (L.) Vill.- A plant with immense therapeutic potentials: phytochemistry and pharmacology. *Heliyon*, 6(6), e04150. https://doi.org/10.1016/j.heliyon.2020.e04150

Oregon Grape - Mahonia aquifolium - PNW Plants. (n.d.). Copyright (C) 2006 Filaret Ilas. All Rights Reserved. http://www.pnwplants.wsu.edu/PlantDisplay.aspx?PlantID=299

Oregon White Oak - Quercus garryana - PNW Plants. (n.d.). Copyright (C) 2006 Filaret Ilas. All Rights Reserved. http://www.pnwplants.wsu.edu/PlantDisplay.aspx?PlantID=295

OregonFlora. (n.d.). https://oregonflora.org/taxa/garden.php?taxon=6408

Pan, J., Wang, H., & Chen, Y. (2022). Prunella vulgaris L. – A Review of its Ethnopharmacology, Phytochemistry, Quality Control and Pharmacological Effects. *Frontiers in Pharmacology*, 13. https://doi.org/10.3389/fphar.2022.903171

Picea sitchensis | Landscape Plants | Oregon State University. (n.d.). https://landscapeplants.oregonstate.edu/plants/picea-sitchensis

Picea sitchensis (Coast Spruce, Sitka Spruce, Tideland Spruce) | North Carolina Extension Gardener Plant Toolbox. (n.d.). https://plants.ces.ncsu.edu/plants/picea-sitchensis/

Picea sitchensis Sitka Spruce PFAF Plant Database. (n.d.). https://pfaf.org/user/Plant.aspx?LatinName=Picea+sitchensis

Pinus contorta. (n.d.). https://www.wnps.org/native-plant-directory/192:pinus-contorta

Pinus contorta Beach Pine, Lodgepole pine, Bolander beach pine, Beach pine, Sierra lodgepole pine, Yukon pine, Shor PFAF Plant Database. (n.d.). https://pfaf.org/user/Plant.aspx?LatinName=Pinus+contorta

Pinus contorta var. contorta | Landscape Plants | Oregon State University. (n.d.). https://landscapeplants.oregonstate.edu/plants/pinus-contorta-var-contorta

PLANTS Profile for Rubus allegheniensis (Allegheny blackberry) | USDA PLANTS. (2023, March 15). https://adminplants.sc.egov.usda.gov/java/profile?symbol=RUAL&photoID=rual_009_avp.jpg

Polygonum bistortoides American Bistort PFAF Plant Database. (n.d.). https://pfaf.org/User/Plant.aspx?LatinName=Polygonum+bistortoides

Populus trichocarpa | Landscape Plants | Oregon State University. (n.d.). https://landscapeplants.oregonstate.edu/plants/populus-trichocarpa

Populus trichocarpa Western Balsam Poplar, Black cottonwood PFAF Plant Database. (n.d.). https://pfaf.org/user/Plant.aspx?LatinName=Populus+trichocarpa

Portulaca oleracea (Common Purslane, Garden Purslane, Little Hogweed, Little Hog Weed, Moss Rose, Pigweed, Pigweed, Portulaca, Purselane, Purslane, Pusley, Red Root, Rock Moss, Verdolaga, Wild Portulaca) | North Carolina Extension Gardener Plant Toolbox. (n.d.). https://plants.ces.ncsu.edu/plants/portulaca-oleracea/

Portulaca oleracea Green Purslane, Little hogweed PFAF Plant Database. (n.d.). https://pfaf.org/user/plant.aspx?LatinName=Portulaca+oleracea

Prunella vulgaris (Heal All, Selfheal) | North Carolina Extension Gardener Plant Toolbox. (n.d.-a). https://plants.ces.ncsu.edu/plants/prunella-vulgaris/

Prunella vulgaris (Heal All, Selfheal) | North Carolina Extension Gardener Plant Toolbox. (n.d.-b). https://plants.ces.ncsu.edu/plants/prunella-vulgaris/

Prunus emarginata. (n.d.). https://www.wnps.org/native-plant-directory/207-prunus-emarginata

Prunus emarginata | Landscape Plants | Oregon State University. (n.d.). https://landscapeplants.oregonstate.edu/plants/prunus-emarginata

Prunus emarginata Bitter Cherry PFAF Plant Database. (n.d.). https://pfaf.org/user/Plant.aspx?LatinName=Prunus+emarginata

Prunus virginiana demissa Western Chokecherry PFAF Plant Database. (n.d.). https://pfaf.org/user/Plant.aspx?LatinName=Prunus+virginiana+demissa

Prunus virginiana var. demissa | Landscape Plants | Oregon State University. (n.d.). https://landscapeplants.oregonstate.edu/plants/prunus-virginiana-var-demissa#:~:text=demissa,-Prunus%20virginiana%20var&text=Deciduous%2C%20thicket%20forming%20shrub%2C%20-mostly,Common%20or%20Eastern%20Chokecherry%20%5BP.

Purslane: Pictures, Flowers, Leaves & Identification | Portulaca oleracea. (n.d.). https://www.ediblewildfood.com/purslane.aspx

Quercus garryana | Landscape Plants | Oregon State University. (n.d.). https://landscapeplants.oregonstate.edu/plants/quercus-garryana

Quercus garryana Oregon White Oak, Garry Oak PFAF Plant Database. (n.d.). https://pfaf.org/user/Plant.aspx?LatinName=Quercus+garryana

R. (2013, July 29). Rubus allegheniensis | CLIMBERS. https://climbers.lsa.umich.edu/?p=1061

Raeeszadeh, M., Beheshtipour, J., Jamali, R., & Akbari, A. (2022). The Antioxidant Properties of Alfalfa (Medicago sativa L.) and Its Biochemical, Antioxidant, Anti-Inflammatory, and

Pathological Effects on Nicotine-Induced Oxidative Stress in the Rat Liver. *Oxidative Medicine and Cellular Longevity*, 2022, 1–13. https://doi.org/10.1155/2022/2691577

Red Clover. (n.d.). NCCIH. https://www.nccih.nih.gov/health/red-clover

Ribes divaricatum | Landscape Plants | Oregon State University. (n.d.). https://landscapeplants.oregonstate.edu/plants/ribes-divaricatum

Ribes divaricatum Coastal Black Gooseberry, Spreading gooseberry, Parish's gooseberry, Straggly gooseberry PFAF Plant Database. (n.d.). https://pfaf.org/user/Plant.aspx?LatinName=Ribes+divaricatum

Robinia pseudoacacia - Plant Finder. (n.d.). http://www.missouribotanicalgarden.org/PlantFinder/PlantFinderDetails.aspx?kempercode=c143%22

Robinia pseudoacacia (Black Locust, Common Locust, False Acacia, Green Locust, Pea Flower Locust, White Locust, Yellow Locust) | North Carolina Extension Gardener Plant Toolbox. (n.d.). https://plants.ces.ncsu.edu/plants/robinia-pseudoacacia/

Robinia pseudoacacia (Black Locust): Minnesota Wildflowers. (n.d.). https://www.minnesotawildflowers.info/tree/black-locust

Robinia pseudoacacia Black Locust, Yellow Locust PFAF Plant Database. (n.d.). https://pfaf.org/user/plant.aspx?latinname=Robinia+pseudoacacia

Rosa canina (dog rose): Go Botany. (n.d.). https://gobotany.nativeplanttrust.org/species/rosa/canina/

Rosa canina Dog Rose PFAF Plant Database. (n.d.). https://pfaf.org/user/plant.aspx?LatinName=Rosa+canina

Rosa nutkana. (n.d.). https://www.wnps.org/native-plant-directory/218:rosa-nutkana

Rosa nutkana | Landscape Plants | Oregon State University. (n.d.). https://landscapeplants.oregonstate.edu/plants/rosa-nutkana

Rosa nutkana Nootka Rose, Bristly Nootka rose PFAF Plant Database. (n.d.). https://pfaf.org/User/Plant.aspx?LatinName=Rosa+nutkana

Rubus allegheniensis Alleghany Blackberry, Graves' blackberry PFAF Plant Database. (n.d.). https://pfaf.org/User/Plant.aspx?LatinName=Rubus+allegheniensis

Rubus allegheniensis (Allegheny Blackberry, Blackberry, Common Blackberry, Dewberry, Graves' blackberry) | North Carolina Extension Gardener Plant Toolbox. (n.d.). https://plants.ces.ncsu.edu/plants/rubus-allegheniensis/

Rubus leucodermis | Landscape Plants | Oregon State University. (n.d.). https://landscapeplants.oregonstate.edu/plants/rubus-leucodermis

Rubus leucodermis Whitebark Raspberry PFAF Plant Database. (n.d.). https://pfaf.org/user/plant.aspx?latinname=Rubus+leucodermis

Rubus parviflorus. (n.d.). https://www.wnps.org/native-plant-directory/219-rubus-parviflorus

Rubus parviflorus | Landscape Plants | Oregon State University. (n.d.). https://landscapeplants.oregonstate.edu/plants/rubus-parviflorus

Rubus parviflorus - Plant Finder. (n.d.). https://www.missouribotanicalgarden.org/PlantFinder/PlantFinderDetails.aspx?taxonid=286468

Rubus parviflorus Thimbleberry PFAF Plant Database. (n.d.). https://pfaf.org/user/plant.aspx?LatinName=Rubus+parviflorus

Rubus spectabilis | Landscape Plants | Oregon State University. (n.d.). https://landscapeplants.oregonstate.edu/plants/rubus-spectabilis

Rubus spectabilis (Blackberry, Dewberry, Salmonberry, Salmon Berry) | North Carolina Extension Gardener Plant Toolbox. (n.d.). https://plants.ces.ncsu.edu/plants/rubus-spectabilis/

Rubus spectabilis Salmonberry PFAF Plant Database. (n.d.). https://pfaf.org/user/plant.aspx?LatinName=Rubus+spectabilis

Saccharina latissima (Linnaeus) C.E.Lane, C.Mayes, Druehl & G.W.Saunders :: AlgaeBase. (n.d.). https://www.algaebase.org/search/species/detail/?species_id=129132

Salmonberry - Rubus spectabilis - PNW Plants. (n.d.). Copyright (C) 2006 Filaret Ilas. All Rights Reserved. http://pnwplants.wsu.edu/PlantDisplay.aspx?PlantID=280

Sambucus caerulea Blue Elder PFAF Plant Database. (n.d.). https://pfaf.org/user/Plant.aspx?LatinName=Sambucus+caerulea

Sambucus canadensis (American Elder, American Elderberry, Common Elderberry, Elderberry) | North Carolina Extension Gardener Plant Toolbox. (n.d.). https://plants.ces.ncsu.edu/plants/sambucus-canadensis/

Sambucus canadensis American Elder PFAF Plant Database. (n.d.). https://pfaf.org/user/Plant.aspx?LatinName=Sambucus+canadensis

Sambucus nigra subsp. cerulea | Landscape Plants | Oregon State University. (n.d.). https://landscapeplants.oregonstate.edu/plants/sambucus-nigra-subsp-cerulea

Satureja douglasii. (n.d.). https://www.ocplants.org/eplant.php?plantnum=24650&return=c

Seaweeds of Alaska. (n.d.). https://www.seaweedsofalaska.com/species.asp?SeaweedID=18

Selfheal - Prunella vulgaris | Washington College. (n.d.). https://www.washcoll.edu/learn-by-doing/food/plants/lamiaceae/prunella-vulgaris.php

Sidor, A., & Gramza-Michałowska, A. (2015). Advanced research on the antioxidant and health benefit of elderberry (Sambucus nigra) in food – a review. *Journal of Functional Foods, 18,* 941–958. https://doi.org/10.1016/j.jff.2014.07.012

Sorbus scopulina | Landscape Plants | Oregon State University. (n.d.). https://landscapeplants.oregonstate.edu/plants/sorbus-scopulina

Sorbus scopulina Western Mountain Ash, Greene's mountain ash, Cascade mountain ash PFAF Plant Database. (n.d.). https://pfaf.org/user/Plant.aspx?LatinName=Sorbus+scopulina

Southwest Colorado Wildflowers, Bistorta. (n.d.). https://www.swcoloradowildflowers.com/White%20Enlarged%20Photo%20Pages/bistorta.htm

Stellaria media (Birdweed, Chickenwort, Chickweed, Common Chickweed, Starweed, Starwort, Winterweed) | North Carolina Extension Gardener Plant Toolbox. (n.d.). https://plants.ces.ncsu.edu/plants/stellaria-media/

Stellaria media Chickweed, Common chickweed PFAF Plant Database. (n.d.). https://pfaf.org/User/plant.aspx?LatinName=Stellaria+media

Stevens, M. W. &. F. (n.d.-a). *California Fungi: Craterellus tubaeformis.* https://www.mykoweb.com/CAF/species/Craterellus_tubaeformis.html

Stevens, M. W. &. F. (n.d.-b). *California Fungi: Ganoderma oregonense.* https://www.mykoweb.com/CAF/species/Ganoderma_oregonense.html

Stevens, M. W. &. F. (n.d.-c). *California Fungi: Hericium coralloides.* https://www.mykoweb.com/CAF/species/Hericium_coralloides.html

Stevens, M. W. &. F. (n.d.-d). *California Fungi: Lactarius deliciosus.* https://www.mykoweb.com/CAF/species/Lactarius_deliciosus.html

Stevens, M. W. &. F. (n.d.-e). *California Fungi: Lactarius rubidus.* https://www.mykoweb.com/CAF/species/Lactarius_rubidus.html

Straggly Gooseberry - Ribes divaricatum - PNW Plants. (n.d.). Copyright (C) 2006 Filaret Ilas. All Rights Reserved. http://pnwplants.wsu.edu/PlantDisplay.aspx?PlantID=680

Studio Animato (www.animato.cz). (n.d.). *Auricularia - MycoMedica - chinese vital mushrooms.* MycoMedica - Chinese Vital Mushrooms. https://www.mycomedica.eu/auricularia.html

Sugar Kelp — Kombu — Saccharina Latissima — Seaweed Solutions. (n.d.). Seaweed Solutions. https://seaweedsolutions.com/sugar-kelp-kombu-saccharina-latissima

Symphoricarpos albus | Landscape Plants | Oregon State University. (n.d.). https://landscapeplants.oregonstate.edu/plants/symphoricarpos-albus

Symphoricarpos albus - Plant Finder. (n.d.). https://www.missouribotanicalgarden.org/PlantFinder/PlantFinderDetails.aspx?taxonid=278944

Symphoricarpos albus (Common Snowberry, Upright snowberry, White snowberry) | North Carolina Extension Gardener Plant Toolbox. (n.d.). https://plants.ces.ncsu.edu/plants/symphoricarpos-albus/

Symphoricarpos Albus Snowberry PFAF Plant Database. (n.d.-a). https://pfaf.org/user/Plant.aspx?LatinName=Symphoricarpos+Albus

Symphoricarpos Albus Snowberry PFAF Plant Database. (n.d.-b). https://pfaf.org/user/Plant.aspx?LatinName=Symphoricarpos+Albus

Taraxacum officinale Dandelion - Kukraundha, Kanphool, Common dandelion, Dandelion PFAF Plant Database. (n.d.). https://pfaf.org/user/plant.aspx?LatinName=Taraxacum+officinale

Taraxacum officinale (Dandelion, Lion's Tooth) | North Carolina Extension Gardener Plant Toolbox. (n.d.). https://plants.ces.ncsu.edu/plants/taraxacum-officinale/

Tassell, M. C., Kingston, R., Gilroy, D., Lehane, M., & Furey, A. (2010). Hawthorn (Crataegus spp.) in the treatment of cardiovascular disease. *Pharmacognosy Reviews, 4*(7), 32. https://doi.org/10.4103/0973-7847.65324

The BRAHMS Project, University of Oxford, Department of Plant Sciences. (n.d.). *Oxford University Plants 400: Lysichiton americanus.* https://herbaria.plants.ox.ac.uk/bol/plants400/Profiles/KL/Lysichiton

The Editors of Encyclopaedia Britannica. (2023, February 10). *Alfalfa | plant.* Encyclopedia Britannica. https://www.britannica.com/plant/alfalfa

The "Small Chanterelles" (Craterellus tubaeformis, Craterellus ignicolor) - Mushroom-Collecting.com. (n.d.). http://mushroom-collecting.com/mushroomcraterellus.html

Theodore Payne Foundation Store. (n.d.). *Limnanthes alba - Meadow Foam (Seed).* https://store.theodorepayne.org/limnanthes-alba-meadow-foam-seed.html

This is my first test on FB. (n.d.). MISIN. http://www.misin.msu.edu/facts/detail/?id=224

Tragopogon dubius (Yellow Goat's Beard): Minnesota Wildflowers. (n.d.). https://www.minnesotawildflowers.info/flower/yellow-goats-beard

Tragopogon dubius Yellow Salsify PFAF Plant Database. (n.d.). https://pfaf.org/user/Plant.aspx?LatinName=Tragopogon+dubius

Trametes versicolor. (2019, July 3). Midwest American Mycological Information. https://midwestmycology.org/trametes-versicolor/

Trifolium pratense (Cow Grass, Peavine Clover, Purple Clover, Red Clover) | North Carolina Extension Gardener Plant Toolbox. (n.d.). https://plants.ces.ncsu.edu/plants/trifolium-pratense/

Trifolium pratense Red Clover PFAF Plant Database. (n.d.). https://pfaf.org/user/Plant.aspx?LatinName=Trifolium+pratense

Ulva lactuca Linnaeus :: AlgaeBase. (n.d.). https://www.algaebase.org/search/species/detail/?species_id=39

Ulva lactuca (Sea Lettuce) — Seaweed Solutions. (n.d.). Seaweed Solutions. https://seaweedsolutions.com/sea-lettuce-ulva-lactuca

US Wildflower - Yellow Salsify, Yellow Goatsbeard, Western Salsify, Wild Oysterplant - Tragopogon dubius. (n.d.). USWildflowers.com. https://uswildflowers.com/detail.php?SName=Tragopogon%20dubius

Vaccinium parvifolium. (n.d.). https://www.wnps.org/native-plant-directory/346:vaccinium-parvifolium

Vaccinium parvifolium | Landscape Plants | Oregon State University. (n.d.). https://landscapeplants.oregonstate.edu/plants/vaccinium-parvifolium

Vaccinium parvifolium Red Bilberry, Red huckleberry PFAF Plant Database. (n.d.). https://pfaf.org/user/Plant.aspx?LatinName=Vaccinium+parvifolium

Verma, R. D., Gangrade, T., Punasiya, R., & Ghulaxe, C. (2014). Rubus fruticosus (blackberry) use as an herbal medicine. *Pharmacognosy Reviews, 8*(16), 101. https://doi.org/10.4103/0973-7847.134239

Weiner, M. A. (1991). *Earth Medicine--earth Food: Plant Remedies, Drugs, and Natural Foods of the North American Indians.* Fawcett.

Western Choke Cherry. (2019, September 25). Natural History Museum of Utah. https://nhmu.utah.edu/western-choke-cherry

Western Goat's Beard (Tragopogon dubius). (n.d.). https://www.illinoiswildflowers.info/weeds/plants/wst_goatbeard.htm

White Meadowfoam Seeds (Limnanthes alba). (n.d.). Northwest Meadowscapes. https://

northwestmeadowscapes.com/products/white-meadowfoam-seeds-limnanthes-alba?variant=35963754152087

Wikipedia contributors. (2022a, June 21). *Oemleria*. Wikipedia. https://en.wikipedia.org/wiki/Oemleria

Wikipedia contributors. (2022b, June 24). *Crataegus douglasii*. Wikipedia. https://en.wikipedia.org/wiki/Crataegus_douglasii

Wikipedia contributors. (2022c, June 24). *Crataegus douglasii*. Wikipedia. https://en.wikipedia.org/wiki/Crataegus_douglasii

Wikipedia contributors. (2022d, June 24). *Crataegus douglasii*. Wikipedia. https://en.wikipedia.org/wiki/Crataegus_douglasii

Wikipedia contributors. (2022e, August 15). *Sambucus cerulea*. Wikipedia. https://en.wikipedia.org/wiki/Sambucus_cerulea

Wikipedia contributors. (2022f, August 17). *Rubus leucodermis*. Wikipedia. https://en.wikipedia.org/wiki/Rubus_leucodermis

Wikipedia contributors. (2022g, August 20). *Clinopodium douglasii*. Wikipedia. https://en.wikipedia.org/wiki/Clinopodium_douglasii

Wikipedia contributors. (2023a, January 30). *Rosa canina*. Wikipedia. https://en.wikipedia.org/wiki/Rosa_canina

Wikipedia contributors. (2023b, February 17). *Sambucus canadensis*. Wikipedia. https://en.wikipedia.org/wiki/Sambucus_canadensis

Wikipedia contributors. (2023c, February 18). *Taraxacum officinale*. Wikipedia. https://en.wikipedia.org/wiki/Taraxacum_officinale

Wikipedia contributors. (2023d, February 26). *Chicory*. Wikipedia. https://en.wikipedia.org/wiki/Chicory

Wikipedia contributors. (2023e, March 11). *Portulaca oleracea*. Wikipedia. https://en.wikipedia.org/wiki/Portulaca_oleracea

Wikipedia contributors. (2023f, March 12). *Stellaria media*. Wikipedia. https://en.wikipedia.org/wiki/Stellaria_media

Wikipedia contributors. (2023g, March 14). *Holodiscus discolor*. Wikipedia. https://en.wikipedia.org/wiki/Holodiscus_discolor

Wikipedia contributors. (2023h, March 19). *Prunus emarginata*. Wikipedia. https://en.wikipedia.org/wiki/Prunus_emarginata

Wild About Mushrooms: Ear Mushrooms. (n.d.). https://www.mssf.org/cookbook/ear.html

Wirngo, F. E., Lambert, M. R., & Jeppesen, P. B. (2016). The Physiological Effects of Dandelion (*Taraxacum Officinale*) in Type 2 Diabetes. *The Review of Diabetic Studies*, 13(2–3), 113–131. https://doi.org/10.1900/rds.2016.13.113

Wood, T. J. D. a. M. (n.d.). *MykoWeb: Toxic Fungi of Western North America*. https://www.mykoweb.com/TFWNA/P-54.html

Zhou, Y., Xin, H., Rahman, K., Wang, S., Peng, C., & Zhang, H. (2015). *Portulaca oleracea*L.: A Review of Phytochemistry and Pharmacological Effects. *BioMed Research International*, 2015, 1–11. https://doi.org/10.1155/2015/925631

Made in United States
Troutdale, OR
10/09/2023

13558512R00130